Lived Theology

Lived Theology

Impulses for a Pastoral Theology of Empowerment

SABRINA MÜLLER

 CASCADE *Books* · Eugene, Oregon

LIVED THEOLOGY
Impulses for a Pastoral Theology of Empowerment

© of the German original version *Gelebte Theologie. Impulse für eine Pastoraltheologie des Empowerments*, 2019 Theologischer Verlag Zürich.

Cascade Books
An Imprint of Wipf and Stock Publishers
199 W. 8th Ave., Suite 3
Eugene, OR 97401

www.wipfandstock.com

PAPERBACK ISBN: 978-1-7252-7396-2
HARDCOVER ISBN: 978-1-7252-7397-9
EBOOK ISBN: 978-1-7252-7398-6

Cataloguing-in-Publication data:

Names: Müller, Sabrina, author.
Title: Lived theology : impulses for a pastoral theology of empowerment / Sabrina Müller.
Description: Eugene, OR : Cascade Books, 2021 | Includes bibliographical references.
Identifiers: ISBN 978-1-7252-7396-2 (paperback) | ISBN 978-1-7252-7397-9 (hardcover) | ISBN 978-1-7252-7398-6 (ebook)
Subjects: LCSH: Pastoral care. | Power (Christian theology).
Classification: BV4012.2 M83 2021 (paperback) | BV4012.2 M83 (ebook)

04/15/21

For Georges Morand, who instilled in me a long-lasting love and appreciation for the Common Priesthood and whose friendship I treasure.

Contents

Introduction

Is the conception of volunteer work used in the regional church context more appropriate to the modern individualized person than theological discussion of the "priesthood of all believers?" Is this why discussion of volunteers is *en vogue* in church praxis, while the common priesthood is usually only mentioned in historical overviews of the Reformation? It is clear that the cumbersome wording and the theologically laden concept make it difficult to speak about the common priesthood in a pluralistic, individualistic society.

Nevertheless, this concept, or elements of it, need not be in conflict with late-modern society. The question is rather what "priests" and "priestesses" look like today, what kinds of lives they lead, and what form this participation in the priestly office of Jesus Christ takes.

Since Luther's treatise *To the Christian Nobility of the German Nation* of 1520, the common priesthood or "priesthood of all believers" has been among the central concepts[1] of Protestant ecclesiology. Luther emphasized that all Christians are ordained as priests through baptism.[2] Since the Reformation, the conviction that every person can read and understand the Bible for themselves and this is no longer reserved only for clergy has been central to the notion of the common priesthood. This also leads to the conviction that every

1. Unfortunately, this central concept has often been ignored in actual theological work. Barth, *Einander Priester sein*, 15–18.

2. Härle and Goertz, "Priester/Priestertum," 402–3.

person is responsible for his or her religious beliefs and thus also possesses the capacity for theological maturity.[3]

This has implications for theology and ordained ministry. Not only are the celebration of worship and service central to these areas, but so is the lived theology of the common priesthood. Nevertheless, the "holy priesthood" and its everyday theology is and remains a marginal phenomenon in discourses about church development, volunteer work, and in practical theology in general. Ecclesial, pastoral-theological, or church-theoretical considerations do not focus on the daily lived theology of volunteers and their active role as theologians.[4] It is rather in the context of adult education that such matters are discussed. When the common priesthood is discussed, this usually occurs in connection with the rights and responsibilities of laypeople in comparison with ordained ministry.

This, however, is an inadequate treatment of the topic. Instead, it is a matter of how people who have not studied theology can be perceived and taken seriously as theologically productive representatives of lived theology, so that they become a constitutive part of ecclesial and theological praxis. This form of the "priesthood of all believers" requires not only a theological reframing, but also a change in the theological self-understanding of volunteers, in the function of ministers, and in the significance of lived theology.

Thus the considerations presented here will examine the connections between lived theology, the ability of the common priesthood to express itself theologically, and the function of pastoral

3. In the Zurich Reformation, these convictions were expressed especially concisely in the Carolinum Zürich. On this cf. also Kunz and Zeindler, *Alle sind gefragt*, 7.

4. Cf. the SEK paper on volunteer work and in the EKD paper "Kirche der Freiheit" the common priesthood is mentioned, but volunteers are not perceived as theologically productive conversation partners. The homepage of the regional church of the Canton of Zurich is also lacking an association between volunteer work and the common priesthood. Cf. among others Leitfaden Freiwilligenarbeit, "Leitfaden zur Freiwilligenarbeit für reformierte Kirchgemeinden," 7–8; Impulse Paper of the Council of the EKD, "Kirche der Freiheit," 67–68; Federal Office for Statistics, "Freiwilligenarbeit," https://www.bfs.admin.ch/bfs/de/home/statistiken/arbeit-erwerb/unbezahlte-arbeit/freiwilligenarbeit.html.

theology. The "priesthood of all believers" and their lived theology is not limited to parochial church forms or even a return to parochial core structures of the church; rather, the discourse should also include social, digital, and religious networking phenomena. In social networks, people are connected across time and distance, and denominational boundaries are overcome. Furthermore, lived theologies and new leadership structures are emerging at a rapid pace, which points to additional aspects of the common priesthood that cannot be observed within parochial congregations.

In a digital world, the discussion of the common priesthood, lived theology, and their impacts on pastoral theology must be considered both locally for parishes, as well as regionally and globally.

Many people have supported me in the development of this book, stimulated my thinking, and provided helpful feedback. My great thanks goes to Georges Morand, who has inspired me for twenty years, has always supported and challenged me, and has taught me that theologizing should be accessible to everyone. His friendship and honesty have influenced me and pushed me forward. With all my heart I would also like to thank the wonderful team of the Center for Church Development at the University of Zurich, who inspire critical, helpful feedback and a motivating atmosphere for work and research. In particular I am thankful to Prof. Dr. Thomas Schlag and Prof. Dr. Christina aus der Au for their many helpful comments, for pointing out problems, and for valuable feedback. In addition, great thanks are due to many "common priests and priestesses" who have enriched and influenced me during my time as a youth worker and in ministry. Likewise, a big thank you goes to Dr. phil. Jürg Kühnis and my partner Rev. Andreas Bosshard for reading the text from ecumenical, psychological, and practical perspectives, and for their constant encouragement. I am also grateful from the bottom of my heart for the motivating and constructive cooperation at the TVZ. Special thanks go to Bigna Hauser for her constructively critical reading, which has contributed greatly to the book's comprehensibility.

1

Common Priesthood and Volunteer Work

In the celebrations of "500 Years of Reformation" the common priesthood has increasingly become the focus of attention.[1] It remains to be seen whether this is a return to the past or a hope for the future, or should be seen as a phenomenon of crisis in the regional church that is suffering from a loss of significance and resources and a lack of ministry personnel.[2, 3]

However, when the common priesthood is discussed in church circles, the main focus quickly turns to the (social) benefit of volunteers.[4] The "priesthood of all believers" is equated with volunteer work. This is particularly noticeable when one looks at cantonal church websites. There are countless statements about volunteer work, proof of volunteer hours, and motivation for volunteers. In contrast, the theological conception of the common

1. Cf. e.g., Schweizerischer Evangelischer Kirchenbund, "Kulturelle Wirkungen der Reformation am Beispiel der Schweiz," 3–4.

2. Cf. e.g., "Bischof: Kirche muss sich auf weniger Pastoren vorbereiten."

3. Beate Hofmann sees decreasing church resources as one reason that the topic repeatedly gains relevance. Hofmann, "Ehrenamt und Freiwilligkeit," 140.

4. Impulse Paper of the Council of the EKD, "Kirche der Freiheit," 68.

priesthood is hardly found on these websites.[5] Volunteering and social engagement in parishes in Switzerland are usually the focus when it comes to volunteer work that has been performed, and the social capital this entails. From a historical and theological perspective, however, the equation of the common priesthood and volunteer work must be regarded as a problematic reduction. This is especially true if the theological dimension is not taken into consideration.

BIBLICAL AND HISTORICAL BACKGROUNDS OF THE COMMON PRIESTHOOD

Although there have already been many discussions of the biblical and historical backgrounds of the common priesthood, it is worthwhile to briefly outline some of the main lines of thought here. This is necessary in order to properly identify how the understanding of the common priesthood developed.[6]

In the history of religion and in the Old Testament, priests have always been people tasked with mediating between humanity and the divine, and regarded as religious leaders, though not founders of a religion.[7]

New Testament Perspectives and Reception in the Early Church

The New Testament treats the concept of "priest" cautiously. It is used exclusively for Jesus Christ, especially in the letter to the Hebrews (Heb 4–10). The sacrifice on the cross supersedes the

5. Cf. e.g., "Freiwilligenarbeit—ein Gewinn für alle"; "Engagiert im Ehrenamt."

6. Cf. e.g., Härle and Goertz, "Priester/Priestertum"; Härle, *Dogmatik*, 583–90; Walter, "Priestertum."

7. The story of Moses may serve as an example here. He repeatedly served the function of mediator between God and the people Israel. Aaron, Moses' brother, was called by God to be high priest (Exod 28). Eli was also a priest, who assured the childless Hannah that her desire for a child would be fulfilled (1 Sam 1).

sacrificial cult practiced previously. At the same time, through the sacrifice of Jesus Christ, the high priest, any other form of mediation becomes superfluous. As a result, the New Testament avoids using the term "priest" for those who serve in a ministerial office. Instead, all believers now become the people of God and the holy priesthood which brings offerings (1 Pet 2:4–5, 9–10; Rev 1:6; 5:10; 20:6).[8] "Through baptism and faith, every Christian comes to participate in the entirety of the salvific work of Jesus Christ, and thus also in his priestly office."[9] Baptism and faith are thus the foundations for existence in Christ (2 Cor 5:17).

Nevertheless, a priestly office developed again in the early church, which increasingly acquired the function of mediating salvation between God and humanity in the eucharist and absolution. This in turn led to a clear distinction between ordained clergy and the people.[10]

Revival in the Reformation Period

In his *Address to the Christian Nobility of the German Nation* of 1520, Martin Luther took up the idea of the common priesthood once again. Luther established strong connections between the common priesthood and the letter to the Hebrews and Christ as high priest, in whose holiness the faithful participate. In this, however, believers do not simply participate in an activity; rather, their identity is changed, they are clothed in and adorned with holiness: "*Sic omnes sumus sacerdotes, vestiti et ornati eadem sanctitate Christi.*"[11] The priestly existence of the faithful, like their existence as Christians, is grounded in the doctrine of justification and must always be practiced anew: "through the priestly appearance before

8. Friedli et al., "Priestertum"; Sallmann, "Das allgemeine Priestertum in kirchengeschichtlicher Perspektive," 53; Härle and Goertz, "Priester/Priestertum."

9. Härle, *Dogmatik*, 583.

10. Friedli et al., "Priestertum"; Sallmann, "Das allgemeine Priestertum in kirchengeschichtlicher Perspektive," 53–54; Härle and Goertz, "Priester/Priestertum," 402.

11. *D. Martin Luthers Werke*, 40/2:595, 25–26.

God in prayer and through the obedience of faith as a spiritual self-sacrifice . . . since Christians' sacrifice of faith is manifest in love and thus is also done as a service to one's neighbor."[12] Luther grounds the priesthood of all Christians in baptism and faith. One's own priestly existence ought to support others in becoming priests and in their priestly existence. Specifically, this task is manifest in the communication of the gospel in preaching, pastoral care, and confession.[13]

Thanks to Luther, the common priesthood became an important concept in Protestant ecclesiology. Yet it was also employed in the Zurich Reformation. In 1522, Ulrich Zwingli used the phrase "royal priesthood" (*regale sacerdotium*) to refer to the common priesthood. For him, a priest mediating salvation was no longer necessary, since all believers are fundamentally equal before God: "You must be *theodidacti*, that is, people taught by God, not by human beings."[14]

Especially for congregationalist[15] denominations, such as the Anabaptists, who were influenced by anticlericalism early on, the common priesthood is fundamental.[16]

Highlights of the Seventeenth through Twentieth Centuries

In 1675, Philipp Jakob Spener published his reform program "Pia desideria," in which the renewal of the "spiritual priesthood" occupies a central position. It was characteristic of Pietism that the word of God should have an impact not only through preaching, but also through continual reading of the Bible in everyday life. The assembly of the faithful primarily served "the shared interpretation of the Bible and thus the practice and exercise of the

12. Härle and Goertz, "Priester/Priestertum," 403–4.

13. Härle and Goertz, "Priester/Priestertum," 402–4.

14. Zwingli, *Schriften*, 1:146.

15. In congregationalist churches such as the Anabaptist and Pentecostal movements and Baptist churches, the autonomy of individual congregations is given the highest priority.

16. Sallmann, "Das allgemeine Priestertum in kirchengeschichtlicher Perspektive," 57; Härle and Goertz, "Priester/Priestertum," 406.

spiritual priesthood"; it aimed at one's own edification *and in this way the word was meant to be brought among the people.*[17]

Friedrich Schleiermacher, in the spirit of free conviviality, advocated an understanding of the "priesthood of all believers" influenced by Romanticism and the Enlightenment. Schleiermacher's definition is still relevant, since according to him religious communities are formed by the need for exchange among religiously affected people: "If there is religion at all, it must be social, for that is the nature of man, and it is quite peculiarly the nature of religion. You must confess that when an individual has produced and wrought out something in his own mind, it is morbid and in the highest degree unnatural to wish to reserve it to himself."[18] Schleiermacher thus also takes it for granted that like-minded people gather together: "Doubtless persons who most resemble will most strongly attract each other."[19] In Schleiermacher's understanding, every person is a layperson or a priest depending on the communication situation. In this way, people are theologically productive together, in turns, and in various functions.[20]

The revivalist circles surrounding Johann Heinrich Wichern were linked with the reformation efforts of Pietism. Wichern presented his (reform) program at the Church Congress (*Kirchentag*) in Wittenberg in 1848. His aim was the "inner mission" of the German Protestant church. According to Wichern, this renewal could not be realized solely by those who held official positions within the churches. Thus all believers ought to be mobilized by the "inner mission" to improve social and ecclesial circumstances and renew the church. Wichern saw this task as the fulfillment of the common priesthood. He had "in view non-theologians, who because of their professional and social position possess abilities and possibilities that must not be minimized or disparaged in comparison with theological competence."[21]

17. Härle and Goertz, "Priester/Priestertum," 406.

18. Schleiermacher, *On Religion*, 142.

19. Schleiermacher, *On Religion*, 146.

20. Schleiermacher, *Über die Religion*, 270–71.

21. Härle and Goertz, "Priester/Priestertum," 407; Sallmann, "Das allgemeine Priestertum in kirchengeschichtlicher Perspektive," 61–62.

The Theological Declaration of Barmen, the foundation of the "Confessing Church" adopted in 1934, takes up the notion of the common priesthood. Barmen VI[22] is to be read as a commission of the entire community. All Christians are called upon to bear witness to the free grace of God.[23] This task cannot be delegated to academically trained pastors. Instead, the task of academic theologians consists in supporting the community in such a way that they are able to bear witness to the gospel.

The Constitution of the Reformed Churches of Switzerland and the Common Priesthood

The notion of the common priesthood found its way into various church constitutions in Switzerland and is foundational for the self-understanding of the national church. The local and cantonal parish structures, with their model of classification and synodal constitution, are essentially based in the common priesthood.[24] Thus, for example, the church constitution of St. Gallen states, "Every member of the church is called in the spirit of the common priesthood to contribute to mutual accountability with advice, actions, and prayer."[25]

Despite these ecclesial constitutions and the good intentions of church leaders and pastors, the tension between existing hierarchies and the empowerment of church members should not be underestimated. In particular, the professionalization and service-oriented approach that can be observed within the national

---

22. "Jesus Christ says: Behold, I am with you always until the end of the world. (Matt 28:20); God's word is not chained (2 Tim 2:9); The task of the church, in which its freedom is grounded, consists in conveying to all people the message of the free grace of God, in Christ's stead and thus in service of his own word and work through preaching and sacrament. We reject false teaching, as though the church, in human arrogance, could place the word and work of the Lord in the service of some arbitrarily chosen desires, aims, and plans." See "Barmer Theologische Erklärung," Barmen VI.

23. "Barmer Theologische Erklärung," Barmen VI.

24. Cf. e.g., Kunz and Schlag, "Gemeindeautonomie," 71–117.

25. "Kirchenordnung der evangelisch-reformierten Kirche des Kantons St. Gallen," art. 88.

churches does not serve the theological empowerment of the common priesthood. There is a discrepancy between the language of the common priesthood and praxis in national churches and local parishes.

Thus, at both national and local levels, the common priesthood is hardly discussed and is implicitly limited to (diaconal) activities. The theological-anthropological dimension of *martyria* and *missio*, which is inherent to the Christian existence of the common priesthood, is thereby lost. The common term used in the Reformed churches for all voluntary (unpaid) activity is "volunteer work," and people who are actively involved in parishes are "volunteers." With this shift in terminology, the Reformed churches adapt to the usage of other social-charitable organizations and, for example, work that is carried out is temporally measurable and becomes social capital.

VOLUNTEER WORK—SOCIAL CAPITAL

The term "social capital" can be traced back to Bourdieu, among others. Bourdieu distinguishes between economic, cultural, and social capital. Social capital, according to Bourdieu, comprises the "entirety of current and potential resources associated with the possession of a permanent network of more or less institutionalized relationships of mutual knowledge and recognition; or, in other words, it is a matter of resources that are based on membership in a group."[26] When social capital is discussed within the church, this serves to strengthen social status, as it does in other institutions or social classes.

Volunteer Work—A Definition

The following definition is helpful for a basic understanding of volunteer work:

> Free charitable service includes unpaid, socially oriented work organized by oneself or an institution; this refers to

26. Bordieu, "Ökonomisches Kapital," 191.

personal, charitable engagement that is connected with
a regular requirement of time associated with a project
or event, and which in principle could be carried out by
another person and potentially also could be paid.[27]

The scope and development of volunteer work are assessed in, among other things, the *Freiwilligenmonitor* ("Volunteer Monitor") in Switzerland and the *Freiwilligensurvey* ("Volunteer Survey") in Germany.[28] Age, education, place of residence, and background have an influence on one's willingness to engage in volunteer work. The rate of volunteer work is almost twice as high among people with a university degree (33 percent) as it is among those who have not achieved further degrees after compulsory education (16 percent).[29]

Motivations for Volunteer Work

The level of willingness to engage in volunteer work, which is still high in today's society, can be explained by various factors. Since volunteer work does not serve to secure a livelihood, it must be based on other sources of motivation. Many people essentially understand their volunteer work as lived solidarity. An intrinsic aspect of this activity is that it does not need to be performed—it is voluntary and thus not financially motivated. In volunteer work, one's capacity for action and personal impact are elevated since the work is based on voluntary actions, in contrast to work that secures a livelihood. Hannah Arendt refers to this as "action." According to Arendt, the plurality and diversity of the human being is revealed in a person's action, in relationships, and in encounters. Moreover, dignity forms the foundation for this voluntary act.[30]

27. Wehner and Güntert, *Psychologie der Freiwilligenarbeit*, 3.

28. Cf. "Freiwilligenmonitor"; Simonson, *Freiwilliges Engagement in Deutschland*.

29. Wehner and Güntert, *Psychologie der Freiwilligenarbeit*, 10.

30. Arendt, *Vita activa*, 17, 213.

Volunteers fight for what is important to them, for what in part also impacts them existentially.[31] Ultimately, in Aristotelian terms, volunteer work is also a matter of

> happiness in the sense of a 'successful life,' for which we have to renew our efforts on a daily basis and through which society acquires its meaning . . . Employment is only 'half of life,' while volunteer activity is part of life— 'it suits me.' The question of meaning is generally avoided in gainful employment, whereas it is addressed spontaneously in volunteer work, even if the signification is not immediately available to the persons involved, but remains implicit.[32]

Volunteers as a Theme of Church and Church Development

The fact that volunteers are a prevalent theme for church development is a recent phenomenon, which has not yet been adequately treated from a theological perspective.[33] At the same time, however, volunteer work is defined as a characteristic of church by church organizations and regional churches. Thus the Federation of Swiss Protestant Churches (Schweizerische Evangelische Kirchenbund; SEK) states, "Voluntary engagement is a hallmark of church and diaconia."[34] This can also be seen, for example, in a statement by the Catholic Church of the city of Lucerne. It ascribes a central role

---

31. Standing up for that which has an existential impact, in Tillich's words, the "ultimate concern," is in turn close to the concepts of faith and of God, however they may be understood. Tillich, *Dynamics of Faith*, 1–2.

32. Wehner and Güntert, *Psychologie der Freiwilligenarbeit*, 19–20.

33. Thus in the online edition of the TRE and the RGG there is still no article on "volunteers" or "volunteer work": See the Theologische Realenzyklopädie Online and Digitale Bibliothek 012; RGG Religion in Geschichte and Gegenwart; the 2017 book by Coenen-Marx and Hofmann offers a successful theological consideration of the opportunities and challenges. Coenen-Marx and Hofmann, *Symphonie—Drama—Powerplay*.

34. "Freiwilligenarbeit," https://www.kirchenbund.ch/de/themen/freiwilligenarbeit.

to volunteer work and even links the credibility of the church with it: "Volunteers make the church credible."[35]

In the debates surrounding the renewal of the church in Germany, the topic of volunteer work occupies a prominent position. Thus, for example, it was included in the EKD paper "Church of Freedom" that appeared in 2006. Volunteer engagement is called a "source of strength" for Protestant churches that must be supported by those in official positions.[36]

In 2016, approximately 19.5 percent of the Swiss population was active as part of institutional volunteer work.[37] People are engaged in sports and cultural associations, social-charitable and ecclesial institutions. The ecclesial institutions reveal the following figures: 3.6 percent of women and 2.1 percent of men work as volunteers.

The volunteer work of the regional churches is its social capital and simultaneously serves as legitimation when the church tax and its social and political rights are justified and defended. Church praxis cannot be conceived or lived without volunteer work, as can be read from the Protestant-Reformed Church of the canton of St. Gallen: "The people who engage in volunteer work make parishes more colorful and lively. They permeate the life of the church and enrich the church's programs."[38] The same can also be seen in recent studies on work with confirmands.[39] Nevertheless, this interest in volunteering in the church must also be seen as a crisis phenomenon based on diminishing resources.

35. "Freiwillige machen die Kirche glaubwürdig."

36. Cf. Impulse Paper of the Council of the EKD, "Kirche der Freiheit," 67–68.

37. Federal Office for Statistics, "Freiwilligenarbeit," table 1.

38. The recommendation of the Council on Volunteer Work in the Congregation: "Freiwilligenarbeit—ein Gewinn für alle," para. 1.

39. On this cf. also, e.g., Koch and Schlag, "Results from Switzerland," 151–61.

Defining the Relationship between Volunteer Work and the Common Priesthood

In one of my lectures, a student drew a helpful conclusion about the relationship between the common priesthood and volunteer work: common priesthood and volunteer work differ from one another only insofar as volunteer work is the active expression of that which the common priesthood describes. Volunteer work is an active expression of the common priesthood, but only when the theological level and function of priests, namely their ability to "appear before God" independently and to express themselves theologically, is not neglected.

It is clear that in the church as well as in society, volunteer work is a central theme. However, unlike other social-charitable activities, volunteer work within the church must be understood as a spiritual moment that moves within the thematic realms of theology and the common priesthood. Self-understanding and self-confidence are altered when the voluntary "task" is seen as doing and living theology.

DEFINING THE RELATIONSHIP BETWEEN THE COMMON PRIESTHOOD AND ORDAINED MINISTRY

If volunteer work is an active expression of that which the common priesthood describes, it must be understood as service to the gospel, as practiced faith, and also as lived theology.[40] Essentially, this activity is rooted in the Christian image of the human being, in the image of God (Gen 1:27) and justification in Christ. It is based on being accepted and worthy and this precedes all activity and achievement.[41]

Thus *all* Christians are equally empowered to witness the gospel to one another through word, sacrament, and deeds, and

40. The following chapter will discuss the term "lived theology" in detail.
41. Schweitzer, "Bildung," 254.

to "be priests [to] one another" in prayer and intercession.[42] This goes so far that the following conviction became fundamental in the teaching of the Reformation: "The validity and efficacy of the sacraments does not at all depend upon the human qualification of the one who bestows it (its efficacy depends rather on the faith of the one who receives it)."[43]

Ordained Ministry as a Public Commission

Thus ordained ministry does not contradict or limit the common priesthood.[44] Rather, ordained ministry corresponds to an institutional commission to the public exercise of certain services within the institution of the church. Ordained ministry is the commissioning of suitable people for the *public* proclamation of the gospel and administration of the sacraments within the church.[45] These ministries are among the hallmarks of the visible church. In addition, ordained ministry should serve to protect the institution and to protect the communication of the gospel within the church.

The common priesthood is not a propagandistic program opposed to ordained ministers and their alleged superiority, as is sometimes claimed.[46] Such a devaluation of ordained ministry does not strengthen the "priesthood of all believers." Ordained ministry stands in the service of the "priesthood of all believers," it is an office that is conferred, and ordination has "primarily the character of a transmission of authorities and corresponding responsibilities."[47] The acquired qualification for the exercise of ordained ministry must therefore be regarded as a calling, in the sense of an intellectual and social aptitude. This is connected with the claim that the ordained person reflects the mission of the church and is able

42. Härle and Goertz, "Priester/Priestertum," 409.

43. Härle and Goertz, "Priester/Priestertum," 409.

44. Härle, *Dogmatik*, 585.

45. Härle, *Dogmatik*, 585.

46. Cf. e.g., Jakob, "Reformierte Gemeindeleitung," 47.

47. Härle, *Dogmatik*, 586.

to exercise it with hermeneutical responsibility.[48] Ordained ministers are not special dignitaries, and they do not differ from other people in terms of their dignity.

The Common Priesthood as a Concept of Dignity

If ministry or ordination creates special dignitaries, this already implies the devaluation of individuals and of the common priesthood. Dignity is already inherent in the "royal priesthood," independent of ability and education. It is expressed especially in the self-understanding of believers and their theological literacy. All believers are called and commissioned to stand in the service of the gospel. How this manifests itself practically is always dependent upon a person, their gifts, and the context.

It can be observed in the daily life of the church that the inability to express oneself theologically and a lacking awareness of being a priest leads to shame and voicelessness. Counteracting this and creating an equitable, dignifying environment is at the heart of pastoral-theological duties.

If communication of the gospel is the core of the church's mission,[49] the primary duty of ordained ministry is to facilitate this by supporting the common priests in their daily service to the gospel. This is all the more necessary as there is always a temptation to assign the responsibility for communicating the gospel to ordained persons.[50] Maintaining the common priesthood within the parish and the church as a whole is always a particular challenge. This can be achieved primarily when the "priesthood of all believers" is regarded as part of discipleship of Christ.[51]

---

48. Härle, *Dogmatik*, 587.

49. The communication of the gospel indicates, on the one hand, a fundamental dialogical understanding of Christianity's self-communication, and on the other hand points to the variety of modes of communication within and beyond the ecclesial form of Christianity. Cf. Grethlein, *Praktische Theologie*, 1–11.

50. Kunz, "Zur Notwendigkeit einer Theologie des Laientums," 37.

51. Asmussen, *Das Priestertum aller Gläubigen*, 8.

Therefore, I submit the hypothesis that the theological voice-lessness of the common priesthood is also connected with igno-rance of the theme of discipleship in German-speaking provincial and cantonal churches.

DISCIPLESHIP AS A CENTRAL CONCEPT OF THE COMMON PRIESTHOOD

Grace and justification as fundamental reformation-theological markers are central in the Protestant churches of Switzerland, as in many Protestant churches. A church that conceptually emphasizes the theme of discipleship comes under the general suspicion of being pietistic or evangelical, or of generating spiritual hierarchies and *primi inter pares*.

In a society in which people were predominantly members of a church and agreed with these values and norms, it is unsur-prising that discipleship was not a central theme. But in a late-modern society, in which the pluralization of lifestyles continues to increase, in which churches lament their loss of significance and members, and in which knowledge about the substance of Chris-tianity is declining, it is essential to reflect on this topic. In the New Testament, in the Christian tradition, and also in connection with the discussion of the common priesthood, the question of discipleship always played an essential role.[52]

Discipleship as a Movement of Searching

In principle, discipleship is not a specific (theological) agenda, but a way of life and of faith that describes a movement of searching of common priests. Although priesthood is already given to the faithful, it must also be undertaken and shaped anew on a daily basis.

Discipleship describes a process of change that is open to dis-course and is connected with the historical Jesus, with the dignity of being created in the image of God, and with the self-awareness

52. One example is the background and impact of Bonhoeffer, *Nachfolge*.

of being a priest. Behind the term lies an attempt to describe a Christian process of searching and learning in which biographical circumstances, contexts, and life situations are taken into consideration, but which always also remains inaccessible to the human being.[53] At the same time, however, its strength lies precisely in this inaccessibility. Especially the Fresh Expression movement[54] propagates a concept of discipleship that stands in the context of everyday life. In this understanding of discipleship, the transformation of one's own person should bring about change in one's society, church, neighborhood, and friendships. The concern here is with enabling the gospel to be experienced and lived in the world: "growing people spiritually in discipleship, in the likeness of Christ, so active, working out the Gospel in the world and therefore, it should have a real outward looking element, it should be serving the community in a serious way."[55]

Discipleship and Theological Literacy

The debate about the concept of discipleship briefly outlined here demonstrates a high correlation between proclamation and the life of individual persons. The plausibility of the gospel is bound to the contextually lived authenticity of individual discipleship and of the individual being of the priests.

In principle, within the debate over the concept of discipleship, the "priesthood of all believers" is taken seriously and, among other things, theological literacy is supposed to be supported. It would therefore be desirable if concrete treatment of the topic of discipleship, both practically in church parishes and in theoretical reflection in universities, were supported attentively, critically, and sympathetically. Particularly fruitful here is an interplay of the practice of faith and practical observation, lived theology and

53. In Browning's words, "God is always finally the agent of transformation" (*Fundamental Practical Theology*, 279).

54. Cf. among others Müller, *Fresh Expressions of Church*; Cray et al., *Mission-Shaped Church*; Moynagh, *Church for Every Context*.

55. Müller, *Fresh Expressions of Church*, 221; cf. also Williams, *Being Disciples*, 16–18.

theological reflection.[56] Precisely in a pluralistic society, special attention must be paid to societal circumstances in the discourse of discipleship and the common priesthood.

COMMON PRIESTHOOD AND THE INDIVIDUALIZED PERSON

Altered living conditions also change people's (religious) world of experience and identity, and the pluralization of lifestyles continues to increase.[57] As a result, discovering one's identity and finding meaning becomes more and more a matter of personal orientation based on individual experience[58] and is not given through external religious and social authorities. Identity is thus subject to a continuous process of construction and requires a constant personal effort of evaluation involving self-knowledge and self-formation.[59] As Little argues, "Every human being is a kind of scientist who actively tests, confirms, and revises hypotheses about persons, objects, and events in life."[60] In this, experiences form the foundation upon which a sense of continuity arises. Perceived identity is "the subjective perception of one's own situation and one's own continuity and individuality, which an individual gradually acquires as a result of their various social experiences."[61] Zygmunt Bauman identifies these changes of mindset and lifestyle as a process from a modern to a reflective-modern concept of life.[62]

Social-structural change is highly correlated with a change in the structure of personality. As a result, the individual's religious world of experience is changed and influenced by individualization, pluralization, and urbanization. This process of interdependence

56. Müller, "Discipleship," 34–37.

57. Woodhead, "Introduction," 1–3.

58. This insight is not new and was already articulated by Beck in the 1980s. Beck, "Jenseits von Stand und Klasse?," 35–74.

59. Oerter and Montada, *Entwicklungspsychologie*, 292.

60. Little, *Mein Ich, die anderen und wir*, 7.

61. Goffman, *Stigma*, 132.

62. Junge and Kron, *Zygmunt Bauman*, 6–10.

was outlined by Norbert Elias already in 1939. His definition of civilization attributes the long-term change in personality structures to alterations in social structures.[63] Thus in the course of individualization, beliefs and religiosity are both personalized (God becomes a personal conversation partner) and made dependent upon individual experience.[64] The Big Questions[65] are thus no longer answered by a social group or tribal structure; instead, the individual is responsible for answering these questions, and thus also for giving her life direction and meaning.

Young people are not exempt from this task. They must interpret their experiences as meaningful and, if need be, ascribe a religious attribute to them.[66]

Theological Maturity

"The religious flaneur," which the sociologist and philosopher Zygmunt Bauman made a household word in his social analysis, craves a "justification of his life story" that is both realistic and religio-culturally credible.[67] The flaneur lives in the moment, seeking not a life strategy that is without contradiction or coherent[68] but rather a religious assurance for his time and in passing.[69] From the perspective of practical theology, Henning Luther made an important contribution to the understanding of the individualized person with the heading "identity and fragment": "However, when one looks at human life as a whole, that is, in its temporal extent

63. Elias, *Über den Prozess der Zivilisation*.

64. Berger, *Many Altars of Modernity*.

65. The *Big Questions* include things such as: What exists? Where do we come from? What is good and what is evil? Where are we going? How should we behave? Taves, "Finding and Articulating Meaning," 15.

66. This fact can also be seen in the unpublished dissertation of Muriel Koch: "Religiöse Selbstwahrnehmung und Selbstbeschreibung bei Jugendlichen. Konfirmandinnen und Konfirmanden als sprachliche Subjekte religiöser Identifizierungspraxis." Especially in the chapter "Erfahrung eigener und anderer Subjektivität im Glauben."

67. Klie, "Kasualgemeinde," 284.

68. Bauman, *Flaneure, Spieler und Touristen*, 148.

69. Klie, "Kasualgemeinde," 285.

as well its substantive breadth, only the concept of the fragment seems to me to be legitimate as an appropriate description."[70]

Focusing on these changes is not only crucial for an accurate description of society and individuals, but also for understanding the human world of religious experience. In addition, they bring to light essential aspects of how the late-modern person constructs faith and theology and, in certain cases, freely chooses to live her Christianity.

In the horizon of societal changes it is not easy to recognize where the notion of the common priesthood still connects with the late-modern flaneur. However, some points of contact seem obvious: in the Reformation, through the strengthening of the notion of the common priesthood, the responsibility for personal religiosity was transferred to the individual. The individual was entrusted with reading and understanding the Bible, became independent from priestly mediators, and is now capable of interpreting her own life in the horizon of God.

The theological maturity called for at that time is present today through individualization.[71] Also the power of influence demanded then in dealing with personal religiosity exists today and can be taken up by the individual at any time. Common priestesses and priests can thus become theologians. Furthermore, dignity is also associated with maturity: both the dignity of a person in itself in standing before God independently, and the dignity that demands the theologies of the "priesthood of all believers," constructed, lived, and sometimes shared in daily life be taken seriously as theology within the church and in practical theology. It is the daily lived theology in which people's actual constructions of faith emerge.

70. Luther, *Religion und Alltag*, 168.

71. However, it must not be ignored that societal freedom and individualization do not automatically lead to responsible treatment of personal religiosity, nor do they necessarily produce theological language skills and maturity.

At the same time, it must not be overlooked that the capacity for theological and religious self-expression is limited within church parishes and among the populace as a whole.

Nevertheless, the theological productivity of the "Common Priestesses and Priests" should not be underestimated, and changes the meaning and function of pastoral activity.[72] In daily life, in one's profession and leisure time and in parish churches, daily theology is often lived implicitly. By contrast, it can be observed that lived theology is more explicitly constructed and discussed publicly on the Internet in social media.[73] The genesis and nature of this daily lived, fragmentary theology will be examined in the next chapter.

72. Grethlein, *Praktische Theologie*, 5.

73. More detailed discussions on this follow in the chapter titled "The Public Realm of Lived Theology—Digital and Analog."

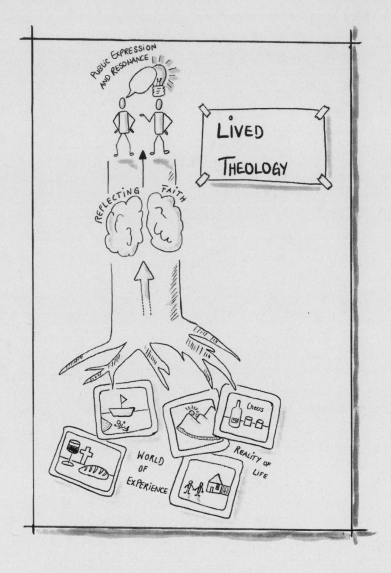

2

Religious Experience and the Genesis of Lived Theology

The term "everyday" or "lived" theology has gained little currency in the German-speaking world thus far, and people involved in church praxis only rarely encounter it.[1] However, it is full-time employees in the church who are most frequently confronted with the lived theology of others and often bring their own form of this theology with them. In addition, there has been a significant increase in the production and construction of lived theology, which emerges participatorily and spreads quickly.[2] This can be seen primarily in digital social networks and online platforms. What emerges from this is that the construction of theology is no longer only the duty and privilege of ministers, church leaders, and theology faculties.

But what form of theology does the common priesthood of today's world contribute? How does this theology arise and what does it consist of? To what extent is the genesis of such theologies

1. One exception is the Catholic University of Saarland's DFG project "Lived Theology in Rwanda's Peace and Reconciliation Process." Here, however, the "lived" aspect of theology is central, but not the "everyday" aspect. DFG-Projekt, "Gelebte Theologie."

2. Grethlein, *Praktische Theologie*, 5.

connected with everyday life? And what role do personal religious experiences play in the individual construction of everyday theology?

This chapter will discuss the development of lived theology in virtual and physical spaces. Research in this area, above all in the German-speaking context, is generally not yet well advanced, and so this discussion should be understood more as an approach to a phenomenon than as a complete discourse.

LIVED THEOLOGY—A DEFINITION

In the German-speaking world there is no fixed term to describe the everyday, experienced, produced, and lived theology of the common priesthood.

In English-speaking areas, people's "lived" everyday theology has been given more attention for some time. Here the conceptions of Jeff Astley and Carles Salazar, among others, have played an important role. Astley is considered a pioneer in the field and coined the term *ordinary theology*,[3] while Salazar works with the term *popular religion*.[4] Pete Ward has recently tried to consolidate various discourses in the English-speaking literature. For the synthesis of *lived religion*, *ordinary theology*, and *The Four Theological Voices*, Ward suggests the designation *lived theology*, which originated with Charles Marsh et al.[5]

Lived Theology in Contrast to Lived Religion

In contrast, there has long been a broad discourse surrounding *lived religion*. In the German-speaking world, this concept has gained currency and been influenced by, for example, Heimbrock and Dinter, Grötzinger and Pfleiderer, as well as Gräb.[6] The term

3. Astley, *Ordinary Theology*.

4. Salazar, "Believing Minds," 23.

5. Ward, *Introducing Practical Theology*, 55–67.

6. Cf. e.g., Dinter et al., *Einführung in die Empirische Theologie*; Grözinger and Pfleiderer, *"Gelebte Religion" als Programmbegriff*; Gräb, *Religion als Deutung des Lebens*.

"denotes a common attitude of searching and not a methodologically unified, shared program."[7] However, behind the aim of "lived religion's attitude of searching" there is a "turning of theology toward a theory of a religious lifeworld, everyday religion, and biography, in which the theories of lived religion can be concretely carried out."[8] Heimbrock goes a step further in his definition when he relates lived religion to the "open process of experience in everyday life." He goes on to say, "And this is specifically about the attempt to come into contact with the pre-reflective immediacy and pre-familiarity of such experiential processes."[9] The authors thus refer to "everyday phenomena" that a person is able to categorize as meaningful for oneself and one's own life.[10] The events and experiences described by Dinter and Heimbrock generate meaning in the life of the individual. But they are not (yet) explicitly categorized as religious by the person themselves.[11]

The term preferred in this book—lived theology—also ties in with the lifeworld and biography of the late-modern person. But it has in view the specific genesis and productivity of theology. This means that the focus is on religious and theological processes that can be consciously shaped and reflected upon by the individual.

Lived Theology in Contrast to Lived Faith

In comparison with lived theology, the concept of lived faith is connected with a religious program. That is, what is experienced or believed by the individual is clearly categorized as religious. However, lived faith lacks the explicitly reflective, critical, and productive element that is inherent in lived theology. In addition, the terminology of lived faith is often found in literature of counseling, life coaching, and Christian or other religious testimonial accounts.[12]

7. Grözinger and Pfleiderer, *"Gelebte Religion" als Programmbegriff*, 7.

8. Pfleiderer, "Gelebte Religion," 32.

9. Dinter et al., *Einführung in die Empirische Theologie*, 73.

10. Dinter et al., *Einführung in die Empirische Theologie*, 73.

11. Dinter et al., *Einführung in die Empirische Theologie*, 74.

12. Cf. among others, Meyer, *Wie man Gottes Reden hört*.

The concept of lived theology created here also contains something other than faith alone. Beyond the faith of a religious person, it also describes the critical moment of doubt and questioning, the cognitive search for meaning and truth, and aspects of the public sphere. Therefore I intentionally use the terminology of lived theology rather than lived faith. For the same reasons, Mildenberger's phrase "simple talk of God" will not be used. According to Mildenberger, "simple talk of God" is supposed to relieve "theology of the task of having to prove its discussion of God to be true."[13] But the lived theology of an individual person usually has a personal element of truth and an individual normativity.[14]

Lived Theology in Contrast to Ordinary Theology

It would also have been possible to translate Astley's concept of ordinary theology as accurately as possible into German. This concept allows for various interpretations, and so "everyday theology," "commonplace theology," or "normal theology" would have been options. However, since the definition developed here goes further than Astley's definition, I have avoided using a translation of this phrase and created my own term with lived theology.

This is based on the following reasons: According to Astley, ordinary theology denotes faith and the process of faith, and it is expressed in the "God-talk" of the faithful who have completed no theological training: "Ordinary theology is my term for the theological beliefs and processes of believing that find expression in the God-talk of those believers who have received no scholarly theological education."[15]

The first part of Astley's definition is illuminating. He selects a process-oriented approach to the phenomenon by beginning with theological beliefs and the establishment or further development of faith on a reflective level.

---

13. Mildenberger, *Biblische Dogmatik*, 15.

14. Cf. the chapter titled "Genesis of Religious Experience."

15. Francis and Astley, *Exploring Ordinary Theology*, 1.

The second part of Astley's definition overlooks two key aspects. First, Astley reduces ordinary theology to "God-talk," that is, to the act of speaking about religious convictions. Second, ordinary theology is made the proprium of laypeople.

When the definition reduces ordinary theology to the act of speaking, this excludes elements that are action-oriented, diaconal, and artistic. Of course, it is characteristic of the term *theologia* that, because of its roots of *theos* and *logos*, doctrine and language about God are in focus. Nevertheless, in the Old and New Testaments, theology was practiced in songs (psalms), symbolic acts, diaconal ministries, etc. If theology is the action that makes the *theos* publicly visible in the world, then the doing of ordinary theology ought not be reduced to the act of speech.

If ordinary theology is a hallmark of laypeople, it contains a strong perspective of idealizing education. Astley's basic definition presupposes that ordinary theology is the theology that is done by people who have not studied theology. But the theology that is expressed in life cannot be reduced, as it is in Astley's definition, to people who have not studied theology, but rather applies to every person who moves within the Christian system of meaning. By making ordinary theology the proprium of non-academically educated people, Astley ignores the fact that, despite a theological education, personally constructed lived theology is also an integral part of those (ordained) people who are employed by the church. Although Astley mentions that even academically educated theologians have an ordinary theology, his program is rooted only in the "laity." In the German-speaking world, the term "lay theology," which is used now and then for the theology of the common priesthood,[16] would be analogous to ordinary theology.

The concept of lived theology removes this reduction by locating this form of theology in the life of the entire ordained and non-ordained common priesthood, which includes both ordained and non-ordained people.

The considerations presented here support the thesis that lived theology concerns all people and that academically educated

16. Kunz, "Zur Notwendigkeit einer Theologie des Laientums."

theologians are not excluded from this. Therefore a division between the theology of laypeople and that of ordained persons is not helpful in this discourse.

Lived Theology as Analogous to Popular Theology

Salazar also argues similarly to Astley, although his definition is more open and closest to the conception of lived theology employed here. According to Salazar, religion is a cultural phenomenon and can thus assume different manifestations and forms. Salazar distinguishes first of all two forms: "erudite theology" and "popular theology."[17] The former is predominantly the work of educated theologians, which can take very elaborate forms in academic discourse. Its function is the research into, preservation of, and contextualized reflection on the Christian tradition and lived religious praxis. This is contrasted with "popular theology." It is shaped by people's life system, world of experience, culture, and context. It is "analogous to language, sexuality or kinship."[18] It is continually recreated by the individual through conscious and subconscious processes. What is proven, certain, and serves life is kept, while other ideas are reconsidered or reconstructed through experience.

Definition of Lived Theology

Lived theology applies to everyone, including academics. It is the essential and existential theology of the individual. In addition, this form of theology is also the one which often shapes church life and the orientation of parishes.

While the conception of lived theology employed here denotes people's theologizing, the form it takes is not reduced to an activity such as speaking or thinking; rather, it integrates other forms of expression such as art and music.

Lived theology describes a phenomenon that is manifest in praxis. The term stands for the common Christian theologies of

17. Salazar, "Believing Minds," 23.
18. Salazar, "Believing Minds," 23.

individualized people, usually constructed personally and integrated in daily life. It refers to an experienced and experienceable theology, one which must prove itself in life and which thus exhibits many pragmatic elements. This terminology integrates private convictions, expressed in any given form, as well as the lived (and reflected upon) practice of faith. Thus the form of this theology is never the security of an answer, but rather a "questioning existence between refutation and certainty."[19]

This form of theology is a processual theology based on personal and communal experiences (of contingency) and is subject to shifts in life circumstances and context.[20] The term describes a phenomenon that is manifest in praxis and is suited to the individual's day-to-day living and world of experience: "ordinary theology in some sense 'works' for those who own it. It fits their life experience and gives meaning to, and expresses the meaning they find within their own lives."[21] This definition must be supplemented by the following point in order to include the entire horizon of meaning of lived theology: religious experience and lived faith becomes theology when it is expressed in some form, when it acquires a public aspect, and is thus at least theoretically open to and capable of discourse.

> Lived theology is grounded in the world of experience and life reality of human beings. It becomes theology when it is expressed with reflection and resonates in the public sphere.

Lived theology is grounded in the personal experience of human beings. The systematic theologian Paul Tillich proposed a helpful definition of the relationship between lived theology and experience. Thus his thoughts serve as a theological framework for the discussion of how experiences first become religious experience and lived theology then develops from there.

19. H. Luther, *Religion und Alltag*, 23.
20. Green, *Let's Do Theology*, 3–5.
21. Astley, *Ordinary Theology*, 2.

DEFINING THE RELATIONSHIP BETWEEN LIVED THEOLOGY AND EXPERIENCE

Tillich's reflections almost fifty years ago already considered the relationship between theology and experience. They are still relevant today for the relationship between lived theology and experiences.

Lived theology develops in the most diverse places, manifests itself in digital and analog form, and is independent of denominations. Nevertheless, its common aspect of creation lies in experience. Tillich never tired of emphasizing that theology is based on experience and derives its legitimacy from it: "The sources of systematic theology can be sources only for one who participates in them, that is, through experience."[22]

Theology and religious experience are deeply interconnected and interwoven. Without religious experience, theology lacks the object of its theologizing. Without theology, religious experience is left to itself without interpretation, or without a conversation partner.

The Contextual Task of Theology

Nevertheless, in order for theology to perform the interpretation that is demanded of it, it must be able to maintain the tension between two poles. It must be a reference system for the historical Christian message and simultaneously its interpretation for the present: "the statement of the truth of the Christian message and the interpretation of this truth of every new generation."[23] Theology is therefore "the methodical explanation of the contents of the

22. Tillich, *Systematic Theology*, 46.

23. Tillich, *Systematic Theology*, 3; Interestingly, there are significant parallels between Tillich's definition of theology and the preface to the Church of England's ordination vows. The ordained priests of the Church of England promise to fulfill in their office this same specific twofold balancing act between tradition and innovation. In addition, it is noteworthy that newer ecclesial and missional movements such as the Fresh Expressions movement connect with this paradigm. The entire ecclesiology of these movements directs its focus and its praxis toward this balancing act. On this cf. Müller, *Fresh Expressions of Church*, 3, 83–84, 181–84, 286–87.

Christian faith."[24] In order for theology to live up to its task, it must be able to refer to the current culture, context, and even the life circumstances of individuals and groups: "The task of theology . . . is mediation between the eternal criterion of truth as it is manifest in the picture of Jesus as the Christ and the changing experiences of individuals and groups, their varying questions, and their categories of perceiving reality."[25] In addition, theology possesses a distinct anthropological function of creating meaning: "Theology deals with the meaning of being for us."[26] In this, Tillich distinguishes himself from a kerygmatic theology,[27] identifying himself with an apologetic theology that provides answers. He emphasizes the strength of this approach: "Apologetic theology is 'answering theology.'"[28] He also elaborates on the question that apologetic theology responds to and locates this situationally: "It answers the questions implied in the situation in the power of the eternal message and with the means provided by the situation whose questions it answers."[29]

In order for apologetic theology to neither lose its truth and language in the present situation nor fall into cultural irrelevance, the principle of correlation offers itself as a practicable path.[30] With the principle of correlation, Tillich attempts to set situational questions with their implicit answers of the Christian message as well as human existence and transcendental aspects in relation to one another: "The following system is an attempt to use the method of correlation as a way of uniting message and situation. It tries to correlate the questions implied in the situation with the answers implied in the message . . . It correlates questions

24. Müller, *Fresh Expressions of Church*, 28.

25. Tillich, *Protestant Era*, ix.

26. Tillich, *Systematic Theology*, 22.

27. Tillich, *Systematic Theology*, 4–8.

28. Tillich, *Systematic Theology*, 6.

29. Tillich, *Systematic Theology*, 6.

30. Tillich, *Systematic Theology*, 6–8.

and answers, situation and message, human existence and divine manifestation."[31]

Because of the correlation method[32] the foundation of Tillich's systematic theological concept is located both in contemporary culture and in religious experience. In Tillich's understanding of theology, theology formulates the questions of human existence, but to the same extent seeks answers to these questions:

> Theology formulates the questions implied in human existence, and theology formulates the answers implied in divine self-manifestation under the guidance of the questions implied in human existence. . . . The answers implied in the event of revelation are meaningful only in so far as they are in correlation with questions concerning the whole of our existence, with existential questions.[33]

The problem here arises when theology simultaneously asks and answers. This program could potentially become stuck in a one-sided deductive normativity. The genesis of religious experiences, however, reveals that the function of theology is crucial to identifying an experience as *religious*.[34]

GENESIS OF RELIGIOUS EXPERIENCE

According to Tillich, existential human questions and experiences are *the* essential conversation partner of theology, with which it must necessarily be occupied. On closer examination, the experiences that are regarded as the objects of theology are given two

31. Tillich, *Systematic Theology*, 8.

32. Tillich, *Systematic Theology*, 59–66. Tillich summarizes his method of correlation as follows: "The method of correlation explains the contents of the Christian faith through existential questions and theological answers in mutual interdependence." In this, three correlating thematic areas are central: "The first meaning of correlation refers to the central problem of religious knowledge . . . The second meaning of correlation determines the statements about God and the world . . . The third meaning of correlation qualifies the divine-human relationship within religious experience."

33. Tillich, *Systematic Theology*, 61.

34. Cf. the following chapter: "Genesis of Religious Experience."

specifications. Tillich points to questions and experiences that have an existential and meaningful character and are religious.[35] These do not lead to emptiness and meaninglessness, but are grounded in the courage to exist, that is, "in the God who appears when God has been buried in the fear of doubt."[36]

Tillich's discussions of the concept of God and human existence are grounded in the conviction that "the object of theology is found in the symbols of religious experience."[37]

Sensory Experiences as Fertile Soil for Religious Experience

Religious experiences and lived theology are closely connected in the late-modern person.[38] Personal faith and individual lived theology are constructed from the building blocks of personal experiences and external impulses: "Religion becomes perceptible to the senses, becomes visible."[39]

This sensory level is not only evident today, but can also be observed biblically and historically. Here one can point, for example, to Jacob's Ladder in Genesis 28, the woman at the well in John 4, Paul's experience on the road to Damascus in Acts 9 and Galatians 1, Martin Luther's Tower Experience, or Bonhoeffer's reflections and poems[40] in prison.

Religious experience is a very personal topic. At the same time, there is limited knowledge and education about religious traditions and interpretive possibilities. People who are especially young are often unable to draw on a preformed religious narrative. And religious experiences do not automatically occur in church spaces. A classroom, the living room, a YouTube video, a concert,

35. Stenger, "Faith (and Religion)," 103.

36. Tillich, *Der Mut zum Sein*, 139.

37. Tillich, "Theology and Symbolism," 108.

38. The German language uses different words to distinguish between a person's "experience" as that which is lived through (*Erleben/Erlebnis*) and "experience" as the sum of practical knowledge gained from one's lived experiences (*Erfahrung*).

39. Failing and Heimbrock, *Gelebte Religion wahrnehmen*, 248.

40. Cf. e.g., Bonhoeffer, "Wer bin ich."

a chat room, the mountains, a hospital stay, or a campfire can become a religious experience.[41]

Religious experiences are subjective, but this does not diminish their truth content for the individual person.

When religious experiences take place in an everyday setting they are much more difficult to put into words, since the language of ecclesial settings is not accessible to young people. In addition, these experiences are not subject to any conscious hermeneutics given by the setting.

Causes of a Religious Interpretation of Everyday Experiences

But how do these religious experiences, which form the basis of lived theology, come to be? Why do certain experiences shape one's life in the long term while others do not? Qualitative surveys for my postdoctoral project[42] revealed three levels of action and five to seven qualities that are necessary for something to be given the attribute "religious."

A religious experience often manifests itself in everyday situations. However, it does not drift untethered in space. An essential feature is that the attribution of the religious does not occur through an external form, a specific ecclesial setting, or a certain religious practice. Rather, the hallmark is that the experience meets with a (religious) resonant space. This usually occurs subconsciously, but is accomplished through three levels (of action): experience of

41. On this cf. e.g., the hashtag #ReligiousExperience on Twitter: "I'm still processing what it meant to finally see Beyoncé live in concert. Thank you @llovellin for the best birthday present a gal could ask for. #OTRII #religiousexperience"; "A gazillion thanks to the folks at Levon Helm Studios in Woodstock for letting me sneak in yesterday and play 'I Shall Be Released' on Richard Manuel's piano. #ReligiousExperience"; "When I die, bury me in the #Twombly room at @philamuseum #ReligiousExperience #CyTwombly #Philadel-phiaMuseumofArt." And cf. also among others Green, *Let's Do Theology*, 5.

42. The research results mentioned here are also found in Müller, "How Ordinary Moments Become Religious Experiences," 79–96.

minor/major contingency; relational religious impulses; personal movements of searching.

1. *Experience of contingency*: Surprisingly, the inaccessibility of life is discussed with people in all datasets collected thus far. The experience of the fundamental openness and lack of control of the human experience of life is an essential activating factor. The experience of contingency among young people is diverse and complex; fears about the future, everyday difficulties, self-doubt, questioning of one's system of origin and values, as well as divorce and illness, fear of loss, and psychological problems are discussed.

2. *Relational religious impulses*: In every case, people who speak of religious experience have at some point acquired religious impulses which they felt spoke to them directly.[43] In this, external religious impulses encounter a resonant space in the biography and/or emotionality of the individual. These impulses are not always immediately apparent and can differ greatly depending on the context. Religious relational impulses can, among other things, stem from television programs and sermons, music, social media, platonic relationships, peers, books, seminars, pastors, or family influence. In addition, the impulses for young people that stem from positive experiences in religious education and confirmation classes should not be underestimated. Explicit and implicit Christian education processes can be observed in all cases. The impulses themselves are diverse and dependent upon each person and personality, but in all cases they have supported or triggered in the individual a movement of searching that is more implicit than explicit.

3. *Personal movement of searching*: The personal movement of searching is decisive for the development of religious

---

43. Engaged church members often and repeatedly draw these impulses from the church community: from their involvement, from volunteer opportunities and training, children's or adult church camps, house meetings, discussion groups, immigrant work, and worship services.

experience. It is based on an active approach to experiences and situations of contingency. In crises, questions, and uncertainty, an open attitude of expectation can be observed in people with religious experiences. This can, but need not, be specifically directed toward a divine conversation partner. In any case, the movement of searching is found in the expectation of discovering something inaccessible or transcendent.

The three levels of action thus consist of an inaccessible part (contingency), a relational part (the other, God, external impulses), and a self-motivational part (movement of searching). It is specific to all levels of action that they refer to the Big Questions[44] repeatedly and from various perspectives and positions, but these do not always align with a personal system of meaning.

However, the three levels of action alone are not enough to render an everyday experience a special event that can be associated with a religious system of meaning. Although these experiences are characterized by subjectivity, there are common qualitative factors in life histories that are shared by all religious experiences. When one analyzes the individual definitions and statements about religious experience systematically, it becomes apparent that five to seven aspects are regularly repeated in these experiences:

- *Needs*: Religious experiences are linked with personal needs, questions, and difficulties, i.e., with existential dimensions of life. In everyday religious experience, existential and emotional needs are often satisfied.

- *Feelings*: Religious experiences also always have emotional and physical components. No everyday experience is designated as religious unless emotions are also triggered. Thus people speak about feeling warmth during the experience, crying, feeling loved, getting goosebumps, being happy, feeling safe and secure, etc.

44. Taves, "Finding and Articulating Meaning in Secular Experience," 15–17.

- *Relationality*: Religious experiences are experiences of relationship. They reflect the subject back upon itself (self-relationship), but are facilitated or influenced by other persons and, in terms of the participants, always stand in relation to language of transcendence.

- *The holy—God*: A transcendental aspect is inherent to experiences that are categorized within the Christian system of meaning; they cannot be conceived without this aspect. Only the terminology used for transcendence varies.

- *Intuitive knowledge*: Religious experiences give the subject new insight. This is not a matter of cognitive expertise; rather, subjects describe an intuitive knowledge they have gained that cannot be easily grasped. People have been shown to be aware that this intuitive knowledge is subjective and applies to them personally. Thus the intuitive knowledge is more of a certainty than the kind of knowledge acquired in school. It is knowledge based on experience that leads to firm convictions about life and possibilities for action. It is a form of knowledge that has a strong impact on daily life. It is experienced knowledge that has proven to be life-enhancing, life-serving, and useful, and unleashes the power to shape one's life.

- *Dissolution of limitation and the inability to act*: Religious experiences have the quality of leading a person out of, or overcoming, their own limitation and inability to act. They offer options, insights, answers, and solutions for internal and external conflicts and answers to the Big Questions. A religious experience increases a person's capacity for action: the person makes minor or major changes in their life.

- *Change*: A religious experience triggers changes; it contains a life-changing dimension and one's personal system of meaning changes. The change begins with the person themselves, but also has an impact on their environment, other people, and their personal worldview. Thus, for example, self-esteem is strengthened, a perspective of hope is opened, and tolerance is promoted.

Since the processes occurring at the various levels of action are not consciously made by the individual, although the level of activity is high, religious everyday experiences are unexpected and surprising. From the external perspective of the researcher, however, processual typologies can be identified that allow the religious reframing of experiences to be anticipated, at least in part.

When the three levels of action and the qualitative factors described above converge, a resonant space is created in which an everyday experience can be transformed and religious reframing occurs. The levels of action are part of life over a long period of time and can also alternate and be repeated. In certain situations, actions are increased. If a qualitatively intense moment occurs parallel to this, experiences can be interpreted religiously and over time can become religious experiences, even if they occur entirely outside of the traditional settings of Christianity, church, or family.

Concrete Examples

The two following life stories drawn from group surveys serve here as examples of this process.

Abby is a twenty-one-year-old student. She studies economics and Russian and lives on a university campus in the Greater Los Angeles area. Abby grew up in a Christian family and went to church with her family now and then. Since Abby began her studies and moved to the university campus, she has hardly been involved in church and is no longer integrated anywhere. Abby feels a lot of pressure in school and repeatedly doubts that university studies are really the right thing for her. In addition, she has suffered from bulimia for many years and has major problems with her self-image and self-esteem. Although Abby is a sociable and open person, she has not talked to anyone about it and has also withdrawn herself significantly from relationships prior to her religious experience. Abby recounts how she was in the restroom vomiting when something happened: "But there was a moment in the bathroom where I realized that if I didn't stop, then I would die. So, I just called for help and cried. It was a voice in my head, like my body did not allow me to throw up again. As much as I tried, it wouldn't let me go. And I knew at that moment that it was a sign or something from God." Because of this experience, Abby began to speak about her problems and started therapy. She mentions prayer as a supportive element in the whole process.

As a child, Kristine, now twenty-two years old, immigrated with her family from Mexico to the United States. She lives in San Francisco, studies French and Spanish in Los Angeles, and is on an exchange semester in Morocco. Alongside her major courses of study she has begun to study Arabic and now would like to improve both her Arabic and her French skills. Her childhood was shaped by the terrorist attacks of September 11, 2001. In her school and in her circle of friends she experiences strong anti-Islamic attitudes. Kristine feels pressure to take a position and condemn it as well. Only when Kristine starts learning Arabic does she gain new insights into this part of the world. During her exchange semester in Morocco, her image is changed again by a specific experience. Kristine is sitting in her room with a Muslim friend, drinking tea and talking. Her friend addresses her Christian background, takes the Quran and gives her a passage to read that discusses dealing with Christianity: "So, I think the religious experience is that I felt like a light—like I put a light here [Kristine points to drawing] I felt like a light had happened and I had recognized something. And I had seen Christian values in the Quran when I was reading it. So, I think that that's what my religious experience was and it really impacted me in the future to be more sensitive."

Gaining Knowledge as a Result of Religious Experience

The experiences of Abby and Kristine are only everyday in terms of their setting. In terms of their intensity and quality, they are special moments. Such moments occur where there is a need for orientation, and sometimes where an oasis in the desert is needed. For these experiences, Salazar uses the phrase "belief in popular religiosity," which is composed of "cognitive, cultural and experiential factors."[45]

Although these experiences have a cultural and relational quality defined by their situation, they are individual experiences that are not spoken about, or not until later. They are governed by the personal hermeneutics of the individual, who is of course always shaped by background, setting, relationships, and specific systems of meaning. However, these systems are resources for the individual in reconstructing their conception of life and their own normativity. Thus the experiences are something very different from that which could be described as church settings,[46] since they neither explicitly nor incidentally develop a public impact, but rather take place in private and in secret.

These observations support Luckmann's observation that religiosity has shifted from the institution into the private sphere.[47] However, this fact also makes it more difficult for people to speak about their religious experiences.

Although most people make no claim to universal normativity for their religious experiences, these experiences do exhibit strong personal normativity. This is evidenced, for example, by the fact that such experiences are seen as a growth in knowledge, forming the basis for action and shaping one's life. However, this normativity is constructed personally, developed on the basis of new experiences, and must prove its worth in everyday, lived existence.[48]

Active engagement with the experience of contingency is guided and supported by an openness to the inaccessible. Following Troeltsch, such religious experiences can be associated with

45. Salazar, "Believing Minds," 23–24.

46. Hermelink, *Kirchliche Organisation und das Jenseits des Glaubens*, 27–31.

47. Luckmann, *Die unsichtbare Religion*.

48. The same process is described by Arnett as "to think for themselves with regard to religious issues" (*Emerging Adulthood*, 212–14).

mysticism, which is characterized by its internality, presentness, and immediacy.[49]

EXCURSUS: THOUGHTS ON THE CONCEPT OF RELIGION IN RELATION TO CHRISTIAN RELIGIOUS EXPERIENCE

Because the concept of religious experience has been widely considered and from interdisciplinary perspectives since James,[50] the definitions and classifications are diverse. In addition, the discourse is determined by all other disciplines, but less so by (practical) theology. This leads to a dualism in which religious experience is classified either substantively or functionally. A practical-theological perspective on the experienced and lived criteria for definition suggests a third option. A purely substantive understanding of religion cannot be verified, at least in the young people's life stories being analyzed. Especially the emphasis on the individual nature of truth evinces a limited claim to normativity. However, a purely functional concept of religion, which excludes, for example, phenomenological aspects, would also fail to do justice to the understanding of transcendence as well to the definition and the qualitative criteria. A purely functional approach calls into question the dignity and the quality of the experience equally, takes too little account of the creative-interpretive process, and leads to "one-sidedness, when religion is reduced to what it achieves for the subject or society."[51] Gennerich and Streib propose a discursive, interpretative definition of the phenomenon as an alternative to the two previously mentioned approaches.[52] The strength of this approach is that it is open to various readings and is modifiable. This draws on Ricœur in its hermeneutic characterization of the human being. The human being is understood as a

49. Troeltsch, "Das stoisch-christliche Naturrecht," 172.

50. James, *Varieties of Religious Experience*.

51. Streib and Gennerich, *Jugend und Religion*, 17.

52. Streib and Gennerich, *Jugend und Religion*, 14.

hermeneutical being that is continually endeavoring to interpret her experiences and construe them meaningfully.[53] This definition does justice to the dignity of the experience and the personal interpretative achievement that becomes evident in lived theology.

However, in this definition, activity is reduced to interpretation and the passivity as well as the quality of the experience are under-determined. The identification of an everyday experience as a religious experience is a personal interpretative achievement. The levels of action that create a resonant space and the qualitatively intense moments, however, consist of both active and passive elements. A religious experience rooted in an everyday setting consists of a direct, qualitatively intense experience that encounters a religiously receptive resonant space and its interpretation. The resonant space is formed by the three levels of action, and is filled with that which absolutely and existentially concerns and impacts the individual—in Tillich's words, "ultimate concern."[54]

A religious experience can thus be interpreted as a relationship of resonance[55] (activity and passivity) with that which necessarily concerns the individual (quality).

But what creates this resonant space in which the individual is enabled to transcend everyday life and construct contextual, lived theology from fragmentary existence?[56]

This very question is addressed in the biblical parable of the sower, which is recounted in all three Synoptics (Mark 4:1–20; Matt 13:1–23; Luke 8:4–15). This parable symbolically portrays how a space of resonance for the word emerges among listeners under certain conditions, and the seed grows and bears fruit. In other situations, nothing happens, the seed withers—there is no resonant ground for growth. This parable articulates an element

53. Ricoeur, *Der Konflikt der Interpretationen*, 23–47.

54. Tillich, *Dynamics of Faith*, 1.

55. Rosa, *Resonanz*, 435–36.

56. On the concept of the fragment cf.: "However, when one looks at human life as a whole, that is, in its temporal extent as well its substantive breadth, only the concept of the fragment seems to me to be legitimate as an appropriate description" (H. Luther, *Religion und Alltag*, 168).

of the inaccessibility that is inherent to the religious relation of resonance as well as to the quality of experiences.

Thus, from the perspective of practical theology, I do not evaluate the truth content of religious experiences, but rather, with Tillich, classify them within an existential horizon of revelation: "Revelation is the manifestation of what concerns us ultimately. The mystery which is revealed is of ultimate concern to us because it is the ground of our being."[57] Religious experience is what it is for the individual: a qualitatively intense relationship of resonance with immanent and transcendent aspects.

Following Anselm of Canterbury (*fides quaerens intellectum*), and with a view to today's experiential paradigm, we could speak of "religious experience that seeks insight and expression."

If this experience is expressed publicly and takes on a concrete, performative form, it becomes lived theology.

57. Tillich, *Systematic Theology*, 110.

3

The Public Realm of Lived
Theology—Digital and Analog

The processes of individuals just described occur not only intuitively but also reflectively. When these intuitive-reflective experiences, whatever form they might take, find expression, moments of lived theology come into being. Something internal, experienced, and private becomes something public, is transformed into theology. As soon as the religious experience moves from a private, internal sphere into public space and is expressed in art, music, activities, actions, discussions, or words, in digital or analog form, and influences another person, a context, or a (virtual) space, lived theology comes into being.

In concrete terms, then, religious experience becomes lived theology when it encounters a resonant space beyond the individual.[1] Thomas Schlag classifies the concept of the "public sphere" as follows, drawing on the notion of organization and for church theory:

> Wherever a certain organization presents itself publicly
> or operates with a claim to public influence"[2] many of

1. Rosa, *Resonanz*, 435–37.
2. Schlag, "Öffentlichkeit 4.0," 322–23.

the following basic dimensions and sub-aspects are apparent: in the basic dimension of "appearance" these are visibility, profile, and space; in the basic dimension of "praxis," they are communication and speech, discursive interaction and participation; in the basic dimension of "authorities," aspects such as legitimation, power, and authority are central; in the basic dimension of "observation," transparency, control, and supervision; and in the basic dimension of "objectives" of engaging the public realm, aspects of relevance, sustainability, and vision come into view.[3]

I propose that aspects of this concept of the public sphere are likewise central for the genesis of lived theology, since visibility, profile, and space are also apparent in the "appearance" of lived theology. Its "praxis" consists of speech, discursive interaction, and participation, but audiovisual communication must also be added to this. In its public dimension, lived theology poses the question of legitimation, power, and authority, above all in its personal and life-serving perspectives. Likewise, lived theology demonstrates aspects of "observation" such as the question of transparency and aspects of "objectives" in the sense of personal relevance, sustainability, and vision (as the production of meaning).

We can once again recall here the definition of lived theology seen in the last chapter: Lived theology is grounded in the world of experience and the lived reality of human beings. It becomes theology when it is given a considered expression and resonates in the public sphere.

This public aspect is constitutive for lived theology. The concept of the public sphere has been widely discussed in recent scholarship.[4] For the reflections presented here, the following condensed definition is appropriate: the concept of the "public sphere" is

> not primarily the aspect of arousal of attention in media
> or simply the marketplace of various political interests.

3. Schlag, "Öffentlichkeit 4.0," 322–23.
4. Cf. e.g., Grümme, *Aufbruch in die Öffentlichkeit?*, 49–170.

Rather, in the sense of Habermas, it designates the sphere of societal formation in which various agents and institutions with their own profiles and intentions engage with objectives so as to decisively influence this sphere discursively through their own respective interpretation of reality.[5]

When the concept of theology is connected with the public resonant space, digital networking and the digital public sphere must be considered. First, however, the specific situation in church parishes ought to be discussed, before the digital aspects of the genesis of lived theology are addressed in detail.

THE PUBLIC NATURE OF LIVED THEOLOGY IN PARISHES

The various lived theologies become visible within parishes through the public impact of engaged congregation members (and ministry personnel), such as in volunteer work. In this, lived theologies are constructed from personal religious experiences as well as from the "congregational theology." Browning, Osmer, Härle, and many others also understand individual churches as subsystems in the larger church which allow different aspects of theology to be perceived and reflected upon.[6] Recently, particularly in the field of ordinary theology, these subsystems have been examined for their individual approaches to theological questions.[7] This examination has shown that churches or church groups are able to create not only an individual, but also a communal lived theology. The lived theology of a parish takes shape, for example, in various forms of worship services, in volunteer work, in sermons, perhaps in house meetings or conversation groups and other ministries. The parish thus becomes an individual with its own lived theology.

5. Schlag, *Öffentliche Kirche*, 15.

6. Cf. among others Browning, *Fundamental Practical Theology*; Härle et al., *Wachsen gegen den Trend*; Osmer, *Practical Theology*.

7. Cf. e.g., Armstrong, "Some Ordinary Theology of Assisted Dying," 39–53.

It is no secret that, even in a parochially structured church, the members of a certain parish also turn to other congregations, led by a feeling of being at home theologically and communally. Especially in the case of "well-known" churches and megachurches, the theological agenda and its lived theology are also publicly known and thus draw people who are attracted to them.[8]

However, it must be noted that the lived theology of a parish need not be congruent with that of an individual church member. Alongside the influence of a parish, the lived theology of an individual church member is influenced by the media through advertisements and television series, such as *The Simpsons*.[9] In addition, the sports and advertising industries increasingly use religious symbols, language, and interpretation.

In many places, lived theology is apparent and visible much more broadly than just in a specific church context. Many religious people no longer locate themselves within a specific parish context.[10] Their lived theology reveals itself in daily action and speech, in discussing and reflecting both in analog form and on social media.

THE DIGITAL PUBLIC NATURE OF LIVED THEOLOGY

The parish is only one of countless spaces in which lived theology manifests itself and becomes recognizable.

A recent phenomenon, for example, is that people with a Christian background and whose convictions live in this system of meaning nevertheless no longer feel that they belong in any parish that they might like to join. Their religiosity plays itself out outside of traditional institutions. In addition, there are people who are

8. Cf. e.g., Willow Creek Community Church's homepage at www. willowcreek.org/; Saddleback Church's homepage at http://saddleback.com/; Hillsong Church's homepage at https://hillsong.com/; and HTB Church's "Related Churches" page at www.htb.org.uk/about-htb/related-churches.

9. Pinsky, *Gospel According to the Simpsons*.

10. Cf. e.g., Zulehner, "Religion ja—Kirche nein?," 11–31.

active in Christian communities, but demonstrate a strong Internet presence that is theologically productive.

Both groups of people are active players in digital theological discourse. The first are often largely on their own and incorporate digital networks in constructing their lived theology.

For example, on Instagram and Pinterest, many people are theologically productive in the digital realm as a matter of course: "There are new and emergent centers and sectors of authority, rooted in their ability to find audiences, to plausibly invigorate or invite practice, and to direct attention."[11] Precisely the field of digital theological productivity is in need of further in-depth research, as this is a new and fluid field.

Nevertheless, it can be observed that there has long been strong networking online.[12] Often these social networks have various levels of commitment at their disposal. Affiliation with these groups is defined by participation and identification rather than formal membership. The relationships in social networks are flexible, and connection is established by needs, preference, shared values, and (biographical) identification.[13]

Especially in the digital realm, the individual acquires "dynamic freedom of a self-selected interpretative praxis with regard to religious content, signification of symbols, ritual praxis, and individual value preferences."[14] But, as has been shown, the genesis of lived theology involves a resonant space or resonant body. Interpretative praxis in the virtual realm does not take place on a tabula rasa. The hermeneutics of religious experiences and lived theology occur, at least in part, in dialogue with other (digital) friends in social networks.

This means that in a digitalized, pluralistic society, individual religious interpretations of experiences and of lived theology

11. Hoover, "Religious Authority in the Media Age," 10.

12. Similar dynamics of lived community in digital and analog form can also be observed in other movements such as veganism, animal equality, or LGBT networks.

13. Cf. Campbell and Garner, *Networked Theology*, 64–67.

14. Schlag, "Öffentlichkeit 4.0," 321.

develop not only in the context of personal encounters in the analog world, but also in digital networks.[15]

This raises many fundamental questions, and the paradigm of parish churches and academic theology as the hub and center of the genesis of theology is called into question: What kind of theology comes into existence in the virtual realm, and how does this occur? Does this differ significantly from lived theology in the analog realm? What understandings of scholarship underlie this? How do interactions within a virtual community take shape? Do authorities with a prerogative of interpretation emerge? What does this authority depend on? How virtual are these communities and how much embodiment—i.e., physically experienceable closeness—do they need in order to secure their existence, to accomplish religious interpretations, and to develop further? Does virtuality only exist in physical distance or does it become a characteristic feature of such a community?

It can be observed that people engage in relevant discourses according to individual religious interests, and a communal lived theology emerges in this context. This theology is influenced by the interpretation of a certain network, but it is publicly accessible to everyone and has now found its way into the reform processes of regional churches (e.g., through Twitter).[16]

In addition, it can be observed that especially digital social networks form and offer platforms in which lived theologies are constructed. The construction of theology is no longer left only to academically educated theologians, but is intentionally encouraged on social media. Thus spiritual and religious discourses are among the common topics on social medial and have become widespread. In addition, in this space the boundary between the

15. Cf. e.g., *Vom Wandern und Wundern* ("On Wandering and Wondering") by the ecumenical movement Kirchehoch2. The book reads like an individual-communal confessional document. In the individual, sometimes very personal, contributions, however, the common agenda repeatedly emerges. Herrmann and Bils, *Vom Wandern und Wundern*.

16. On this example, cf. the hashtag #DigitaleKirche on Twitter: https://twitter.com/search?f=tweets&vertical=default&q=%23digitaleKirche&src=tyah.

ordained and non-ordained has become permeable: "The network can promote flattened rather than hierarchical structures, along with relationships that allow more dynamic interaction rather than being unresponsive and static."[17] Lived theology as specific to the common priesthood lives from this permeability.

The public theological productivity of the common priesthood can easily be observed precisely in social networks.

PRACTICAL EXAMPLES OF LIVED THEOLOGY IN THE DIGITAL REALM

Explicit examples of what such discourses might look like in the Christian context are Homebrewed Christianity,[18] the ecumenical movement Kirchehoch2 (which translates as "Church Squared"), and discussions using hashtags such as #wewonder.[19]

> Homebrewed Christianity: Since March 13, 2008, Homebrewed Christianity Podcast has been bringing you the best nerdy audiological ingredients so you can brew your own faith. You will find conversations between friends, theologians, philosophers, and scholars of all stripes. What started as a reason for Tripp to interview the authors of his favorite books has turned into a community of podcasts, bloggers, & Deacons (what we call our regular listeners) invested in expanding and deepening the conversation around faith and theology. We hope you listen, question, think, and then share the Brew![20]

As this text reveals, Homebrewed Christianity understands itself as a support network for creating one's own lived theology and as a platform for sharing it. Kirchehoch2 can be traced back (at least) to 2006. From loose ecumenical contacts a small regional network developed in the area of Hildesheim/Hannover. This network considered the large processes of change in churches and

17. Campbell and Garner, *Networked Theology*, 14.
18. See https://trippfuller.com/.
19. See "Kirchehochzwei."
20. See "About," para. 1.

began to pose questions together as a community. Initial excursions, study days, and several ecumenical encounters led to the desire to think about a church of the future with a larger group of people. In the year 2013, "Kirchehoch2—the Conference" took place in Hannover. Following this event it was possible to set up a joint office in Hannover/Linden and to continue to follow the trail of their questions. Kirchehoch2 is thus a fundamental attitude of questioning, is influenced by the ecumenism of the mission, is a movement of people who are thinking about a church of today for tomorrow. Kirchehoch2 is manifest in many experiences as well as great and small stories. Kirchehoch2 is reflected in digital and analog ecumenical learning spaces, in various event formats, as well as in publications and materials by ourselves and others. "Ourselves" includes Sandra Bils and Maria Herrmann, the two advisors behind Kirchehoch2. In their work, these two are both a part of one of the two sponsoring organizations. They can often be found in the Kirchehoch2 shop in Hannover/Linden when they are not traveling around the regional church and diocese seeking (and visiting) new forms of church and the people who create them. The team also includes (at least) nine other people. They are employed by the diocese of Hildesheim, the regional church of Hannover, and ecumenical partners. They thus are not located at the Kirchehoch2 office, but at their various offices in order to develop the questions of an ecumenism of the mission in their respective fields.

Digital Networks as Ecclesial Communities

Social networks such as Homebrewed Christianity and Kirchehoch2 are not only virtual, theologically productive platforms, they also take on the function of ecclesial communities where like-minded people connect, support, and encourage one another. One of the recurrent themes in Kirchenhoch2 is #TheGiftOfNotFittingIn—that is, taking alienation in the church as an innovative moment for the church.[21]

21. Herrmann and Bils, *Vom Wandern und Wundern*.

Of course one could object that virtual social networks do not constitute ecclesial communities since they lack the embodiment, the sensory experience of the religious. However, recent studies have shown that there is a close connection between online and offline communities: "online churches are often connected to offline Christianity and the institutions they represent, even when traditional communal rituals and practices (e.g. prayer or Bible study) are modified online."[22] In addition, the separation between online and offline is increasingly blurred, on- and offline are equally embedded in lived reality.[23]

Interestingly, digital Christian networking communities often exhibit an on- and offline pattern. Both Homebrewed Christianity and Kirchehoch2 show long phases of digital networking and virtual relationship structures which are actualized now and then in embodiments in real life.

Public digital network theology is often made present and given a moment of physical proximity when the digital community actually meets in person. The virtual community thus becomes embodied and physically tangible. The community in the digital realm is nourished by these phases of real meeting, though not exclusively. In the physical meeting the community becomes present and is actualized. On the basis of this analog experience of relationship the community lives on in the virtual realm, until it once again meets physically and is made present. In this way Kirchehoch2 became known through its first large conference in Hannover in 2013. This resulted in a network that spread initially through Germany and has by now extended into Switzerland.

In the 2017 conference w@nder, which was much smaller but more intensely relational, the community was again made present and actualized. A large part of the work of Kirchehoch2 is digital and analog relationships and networking.[24] This work is pursued not only through conferences but also in personal meetings in Germany and Switzerland.

22. Campbell and Garner, *Networked Theology*, 67.

23. Consalvo and Ess, "Introduction," 1–8.

24. Bils, "Kirche2—Eine ökumenische Bewegung," 55.

Homebrewed Christianity also relies on meeting annually for its Theology Beer Camp. One year, the description of this annual meeting read, "In addition to extremely nerdy talks, hanging out with other theology nerds just like you, you'll also be getting some of the best craft beer in the Southeast. And in case we forgot to mention, all of the beer you can drink is included in the price of your ticket."[25] Alongside the official conferences, many meetings among individual representatives also take place in this network.[26]

At conferences and meetings, the network's lived theology is actualized, embodied, and produced; it also gains public attention, for example, through livestreaming and Twitter timelines.[27]

The Recognizability of Digital Lived Theology

The public impact of Christian social networks can thus be quite extensive. Although participation is explicitly desired and diversity promoted, these networks nevertheless exhibit a recognizable theological profile: they can be recognized by their explicitly and

25. "Theology Beer Camp," para. 3.

26. I came into contact with Tripp Fuller and the "Homebrewed Christianity" network in 2016 in Claremont. During my time as a guest researcher at the Claremont School of Theology (CST), I gained insight into the network through Tripp, who studied at CST.

27. From the "Final Report of the Ecumenical Project Kirchehoch2" ("Abschlussbericht ökumenisches Projekt Kirchehoch2") of 2017, which was kindly made available to me by Pastor Dr. min. Sandra Bils: "The medial professionality of the conference in February 2013, for example in the form of a livestream in which the program of the conference was widely disseminated by video in the Internet and thus enabled an interactive participation in the event with 14,000 views through Twitter, Facebook, and text messages, made progress in the three years of the project's allotted time. In the context of digital communication, a permanent homepage was able to be created as an information pool and networking location, which has approximately 7,000 visitors per week. The newsletter, which is sent every three months and informs readers about the project's work, events, programs, and publications, has over 1,000 subscribers. On social media, the Facebook page of Kirchehoch2 registers about 750 visitors per week, on Twitter there are over 1,800 followers, and one video on Kirchehoch2's YouTube channel, with 199 subscribers, has over 27,000 clicks."

publicly produced theology, in symbols, speech, and relationship structures.

Furthermore, it is characteristic that the digital communities and their leaders often present themselves publicly and do so religiously, politically, ethically, and socially. Many such political-religious statements can be found on the Internet, including in the networks of Brian McLaren, Rob Bell, and many others.

There are representatives in these networks who play a leading role and often have a significant presence on social media. For Homebrewed Christianity this is the founder, Tripp Fuller. Kirchehoch2 depends on the ecumenical team that is led by, among others, two digitally engaged theologians, Sandra Bils and Maria Hermann, and is supported financially by the Evangelical Lutheran Church of Hannover and the diocese of Hildesheim.

It is a great strength of Homebrewed Christianity and Kirchehoch2 that the leading figures are team players who are able to engage in public discourse. The responsible people in these networks are concerned with offering space as well as being a place of connection for theologically productive, seeking, and questioning people. The leading figures of these networks aim not only to stimulate theological, ecclesiological, and ethical discussion, but also to take up external impulses and to produce shared, contextual theology.[28]

The networks generate public theology that is specific to the network in social media, podcasts, and print media. Through their large media presence these theological approaches are widely read and adopted. The theological outputs are highly participatory, stimulate new thinking, and also continually point to the specifics of each respective network's agenda. Thus the book "Of Wandering and Wondering"[29] by Kirchehoch2 is a confessional text that specifically discusses the element of seeking, the sense of alienation in one's own religious tradition, and the incompleteness of late-modern theological concepts. The text discusses an existence

---

28. Cf. e.g., Bowman, *Homebrewed Christianity Guide to Being Human*; Leonard, *Homebrewed Christianity Guide to Church History*; Herrmann and Bils, *Vom Wandern und Wundern*.

29. Herrmann and Bils, *Vom Wandern und Wundern*.

that is fragmentary, searching, and interpretatively open. A critical review of the book gets to the heart of the matter:

> The weaknesses of form are to a certain extent programmatic. Nothing is finished here—everything is in flux. It is not a theological anthology in the narrower sense, but rather a document of a theology of wandering and wondering in the tension between alienation and belonging. The word "theology" must not be understood academically as it normally is, but rather literally as talking about God. The book is the manifesto of a movement without claiming to be so and without being a manifesto in the classic sense. Instead it collects a whole series of different perspectives. In doing so it opens up a space without being able to fill it, or even wanting to. It is the space of those 95 percent of registered church members who no longer participate in church services every Sunday. Or of those who do not belong to a church and would never set foot in one.[30]

The theologies of the book originate in the lives of the authors and can be regarded as a fluid confession of lived theology in the network. The discursive, provisional nature of its theology is characteristic of this network—a provisional nature that can always be altered through the participation of others. Even so, due to the two theologians with doctoral degrees and the financial and ideological anchoring in the Catholic and Evangelical Lutheran regional churches, the ecumenical network is aimed at Christian and ecclesial traditions. The network is a playground for innovation based on tradition and context[31] and makes its (theological) insights publicly available to everyone.

At the center of Homebrewed Christianity is the agenda of supporting interested people in constructing and developing their own theology, and providing a variety of ideas for this. The network consciously promotes the process of developing (individual) lived theology. To this end, podcasts, courses, blogs, and discussion

30. Recke, "Wundersames Wanderbuch," paras. 3–4.

31. For the discussion of tradition, context, and innovation in fluid movements cf. Müller, *Fresh Expressions of Church*, 286–87.

forums are offered. Furthermore, Pinterest, chats, Twitter, Instagram, and Facebook, among other things, serve as discussion and networking platforms.

Homebrewed Christianity employs beer brewing as a metaphor for the process of developing lived theology. The metaphor of brewing already implies that certain elements are always required when brewing a beer. If the fundamental ingredients, such as malt, hops, and water, are present, then the beer can be given a unique note according to taste preferences.

It should of course not be overlooked here that the basic elements of barley, hops, and water—that is, the fixed theological foundation—already set the agenda at least in part. Homebrewed Christianity is fundamentally influenced by the "emergent conversation."[32] This can be seen, for example, in Brian McLaren's podcasts.[33] This theology is combined with notions from Cobbs's[34] process theology and postcolonial debates,[35] which in turn raises the question of authority and participation in a new way.

32. Emerging churches are worldwide, heterogeneous, Christian movements that differ according to their contexts and can be grouped in various ways. All these groups share the fact that they want to react to changes in society and see these changes as a new challenge for the church. There is no unified definition of "church" in these movements. The emerging church movement is most widespread in the United States, Western Europe, Australia, New Zealand, and Africa. The term "emerging church" describes a church that is in a constant process of development and is always poised to emerge and come into existence. Müller, *Fresh Expressions of Church*, 53–54. Cf., e.g., http://freshexpressionsus.org/.

33. Cf., e.g., http://freshexpressionsus.org/.

34. Process theology understands the world as a constant process of becoming and ceasing to be. There are no permanent objects here, but rather only events that stand in relation to one another. All that occurs is realized in God, God is the concrete event that provides coherence to the pluralistic experiences of reality. Cobb and Griffin, *Process Theology*.

35. Postcolonialism deals with the end of colonialism and its impacts even today. Despite the end of colonialism, imperialistic structures continue to exist, for example in politics, economics, and education. Postcolonialist theories examine identity, culture, and human groups; they have emancipatory interests and pursue, among other things, the reconstruction of areas of life and cultures that have been destroyed by colonialism. Among others, Young, *Postcolonialism*, 57–58.

Nevertheless, a significant concern and stated goal of the network is to continually expand these ideas and to serve as a stimulus for individuals to create their own theology. This can be seen, among other things, in the various approaches and the podcasts produced by very different people.

Another feature that can be seen in these two networks is an awareness of gender issues. Women and men are represented equally, and are present in leadership, podcasts, and presentations. Discussion is not concerned with role models; instead, political, ethical, and humanitarian issues are connected with theological questions. The leading figures of both networks are intellectual trailblazers with a pioneer mentality.

The diverse production of theology in these networks is guided by certain agendas, is recognizable, rooted in tradition, but is not controlled by the institution of the church. It is a lived theology which is not primarily oriented toward what is "true" but rather what functions in the lives of participants. Truth is defined by functionality and usefulness for life.

It can be observed that this kind of participatory networking increases the ability to express oneself theologically and concretizes the common priesthood. In these theological discourses, with their flat hierarchies, participation and creative thinking are valued and it is not expected that every thought has fully matured before it is expressed.

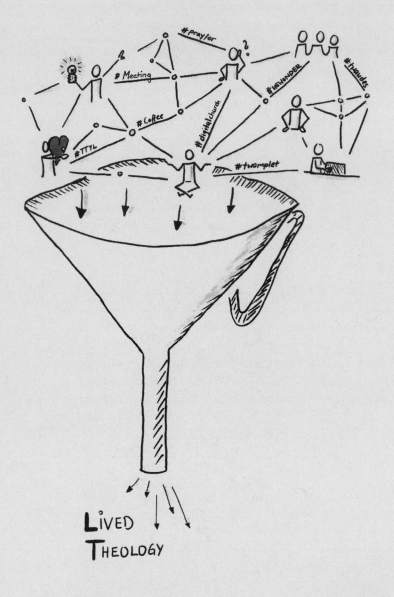

4

Lived Theology as an Aspect of Empowerment

Social media supports people's ability to articulate themselves theologically and provide lived theology with a public aspect. The same thing can occur in the diverse areas of analog church. Regardless of place or space, the moment in which one becomes aware of lived theology, and it is then expressed and acknowledged, has a catalytic function in the life of the common priesthood. In certain circumstances, lived theology can lead to theological empowerment and strengthen people's awareness of their priestly function.

Lived theology is grounded in the context and life of the individual and becomes theology, verbally or performatively, when it encounters a resonant space in the public:

> Alongside the area of responsibility that belongs to ministers, the distinct field of activity for the common priesthood is the life of the Christian in family, work, and society. In this context, standing up for the gospel of Jesus Christ through a lived witness means, in the sense of the common priesthood: to be a Priest, i.e., Christ.[1]

1. Härle and Goertz, "Priester/Priestertum," 409.

There are countless analog and digital examples of this: in church youth work, lived theology often emerges in religion class, camps, youth groups, and social media; among active church members this occurs through various volunteer commitments, or at work and in social spaces; among theologically productive people without a connection to the church, it emerges in self-organized groups and on social media.

When lived theology is perceived and taken seriously as theology, it becomes a catalyst for the development of a priestly self-confidence, for it contains an aspect of empowerment. It is resource-oriented (in contrast to needs-oriented), trusts in the abilities and strengths of the common priesthood, and encourages self-determination and productive (theological) creative power.[2]

In the agenda of lived theology, the supposed difference in value between ordained ministry and non-ordained persons is dismantled. Discussions can take place on equal footing because the concern is not for specialized academic knowledge, but rather for a theology that has proven itself to be useful in life and supportive of life. This chapter, therefore, will take a closer look at the considerations of empowerment, the ability to articulate oneself theologically, the lived theology of the ordained, and the difference between lived theology and pastoral theology.

THEOLOGICAL EMPOWERMENT

The common conceptions of empowerment, especially in social work and psychology, can be traced back to the emeritus professor of psychology, Julian Rappaport. Rappaport's main work on the subject appeared in 1984 with the title *Studies in Empowerment: Steps Toward Understanding and Action*.[3] Empowerment is currently a common topic in the fields of social work, psychology, and medicine, as well as civil rights and women's rights movements.

---

2. Herriger, *Empowerment in der Sozialen Arbeit*; Bundeszentrale für politische Bildung, "Empowerment-Landkarte."

3. Rappaport, *Studies in Empowerment*.

The word "empowerment" means a transfer of responsibility and elevation of the capacity to act. The goal of empowerment is to strengthen the autonomy and self-determination of people and communities, and to create space for creative freedom. One strength of empowerment is its resource-oriented perspective.

In Christian terms, the potentiality of empowerment lies in the doctrine of justification and in some aspects of pneumatology. The idea of the common priesthood is a concept of empowerment, which is, however, always tied to the concept of God. Empowerment and the elevation of the (spiritual) capacity to act are especially emphasized in the Letter to the Romans. The doctrine of justification contains the seed of freedom to live. In the Letter to the Romans (5:18) this is connected with the freedom of each individual person: "Therefore just as one man's trespass led to condemnation for all, so one man's act of righteousness leads to justification and life for all" (NRSV). This freedom is likewise connected with pneumatology in Romans: "For all who are led by the Spirit of God are children of God. For you did not receive a spirit of slavery to fall back into fear, but you have received a spirit of adoption. When we cry, 'Abba! Father!' it is that very Spirit bearing witness with our spirit that we are children of God" (Rom 8:14–16 NRSV).

The common priesthood is empowerment to theological maturity, responsibility, and productivity. With the Reformation's call for individual responsibility and the capacity for self-expression in dealing with the Bible and one's personal religious life, this theological concept aims at people's priestly empowerment. The human being is capable, without a mediator, of shaping his or her life before and with God: if the agenda of the common priesthood is taken seriously, then its lived theology must necessarily be taken into account as an object of ecclesial and academic praxis.

A statement by Rappaport is often cited: "Having rights but no resources and no services available is a cruel joke."[4] This also applies to the common priesthood and lived theology. Even if the phrase "common priesthood" is used liberally, without support for

---

4. Rappaport, "In Praise of Paradox," 13.

theological literacy and without the empowerment of the theology that develops from it, the phrase becomes a joke. Particularly non-ordained people go silent or change the topic when theology comes up in a church context. For example, the dedicated president of a church council recently told me about her experiences in the synod. She recounted how she and most of the non-ordained people in the synod are silent in church-theoretical and theological discussions. She did not have the courage, language skills, or training to articulate her theological thoughts in public. In addition, she was afraid that others would not take her seriously with her faith.[5]

Training in theological literacy takes place much more naturally on social media, through daily interactions. In analog church contexts, however, this presents difficulties. Thus the common priesthood and its articulated lived theology remain only wishful thinking, if they are not actively supported and trained.

THEOLOGICAL LITERACY AND EMPOWERMENT

Even active, dedicated persons involved in synods and church councils lack the theological literacy required to express themselves adequately. There are certainly various reasons for this: despite the Reformation's slogan of the common priesthood, theologizing was nevertheless left to the ordained. In terms of pastoral theology, doing theology and preaching belong to ordained ministry.[6] A capacity for theological articulation is only expected to a limited extent from non-ordained people.[7]

5. Perhaps precisely this powerlessness of the non-ordained is one reason why church committees speak so often about properties, finances, and activities, but so rarely about theology and faith.

6. Cf. e.g., Wagner-Rau et al., "Pastoraltheologie," 111–13.

7. In Switzerland, this is increasingly a problem for full-time, employed deacons. More and more, regional churches are employing people for this office who have no theological education, or have only completed a very limited theology course. As a result, even among deacons, there is only a limited capacity for theological reflection and expression. Thus deacons are able to develop programs for congregations, but not to facilitate the theological

At the time of the Reformation, in the Carolinum Zürich, theological literacy was taught through biblical understanding and exegesis. However, training for theological literacy is rarely found in programs offered by churches.[8] In addition, personal religiosity and lived theology, like the topic of death, have become a social taboo.

As has been shown in some places on social media, the language skills and capacity for articulation of lived theology are again being taught. Theological discussions are thereby de-hierarchized and enable a high degree of participatory theologizing. Thus in the digital realm, subjective approaches to living out one's faith independently are made available. "What and how to believe is clarified by individual subjects themselves."[9]

Nevertheless, and despite the changes brought about by the Internet, theological literacy is only present to a limited extent among non-ordained priests. The communication of the gospel and theologizing are still left to clergy in most cases.[10]

If this is considered from the perspective of early Christianity, the first Christians initially had to develop a language for their religious experiences and convictions, down to the last detail. Christianity spread so quickly because, among other things, it developed a language that people could understand. It developed a multilingualism and translatability of its faith, and this above all through its way of life. The first Christian communities were so interesting for outsiders because they overcame boundaries of status. Early Christianity lived its theology so convincingly that other people were attracted to it. In this process the what (content and

---

language skills and lived theology of the common priesthood. In order to improve this situation, it is sensible to ensure a deeper theological education at this level of employment as well.

8. Exceptions to this are offered by participatory theology courses for adults, specific theological adult education programs, and open-faith courses.

9. H. Luther, *Religion und Alltag*, 13.

10. Kunz, "Zur Notwendigkeit einer Theologie des Laientums," 37.

doctrine) and the how (preaching, living) could not be separated or distinguished.[11]

It cannot be underestimated how central theological literacy and making people literate are to the discourse as a whole. Literacy and the capacity for articulation is linked on the one hand with dignity, and on the other with the personal understanding of oneself as being a priest. Priestly existence is given theologically, but is first laid claim to by individual people who have attained a certain individual degree of making a theological impact.

In biblical terms, creative power lies in the word (Gen 1). This power was granted to everyone (Joel 3). At Pentecost, language was revolutionized. All people preached the gospel (Acts 2). Everyone was allowed to speak.

The helplessness of being unable to communicate and contribute theologically, which can be surmised in the example of the church councils, leads to shame and thus also becomes a form of theological leverage. Thus only academically educated people remain "legitimated" for theological speech.[12]

Already in 1980, in the context of adult education, Ernst Lange pointed to the development of literacy: "We need a language school for freedom."[13] Lange argues here that people's concrete situation ought to be addressed and that adult education should not be exploited for "theological-deductive or ecclesial-structural" purposes.[14] Although Lange had in view a leisure-oriented society and life free of work, this insight is also central for the theological literacy of the common priesthood. But this is not due to linguistic aesthetic considerations, but rather because it leads to a regained theological identity and capacity for action. In discussions of lived

11. These ideas are drawn from the paper by Prof. Dr. Benjamin Schliesser: Reformation als Resonanz. Kontinuität und Wandel in neutestamentlicher Perspektive. Greifswalder Symposium "Kirche[n]gestalten. Re-Formationen von Kirche und Gemeinde in Zeiten des Umbruchs," May 2018, 24–26.

12. Whether this is due to theologians' own claims or an inferiority complex of "laypeople" unfortunately cannot be discussed here.

13. Lange, Sprachschule für die Freiheit.

14. Wolff, "Sprachschule für die Freiheit," 30.

theology, literacy cannot be considered statically or as an isolated event. Since lived theology is in itself processual, language skills can also only be regarded as something that must develop. In the ability to publicly articulate lived theology lies the recognition of its worthiness and an element of empowerment of the person expressing themselves. To discover, perceive, express, and be perceived—these act as a catalyst for the self.[15] And these aspects in turn contain a profoundly priestly dimension. For where God is discussed and the agenda of the kingdom of God can be experienced, theological language skills emerge that are separate from the mere speech act alone, but are life-enhancing and life-serving. The capacity for experience and theological literacy are thus intertwined.

THE ROLE OF PASTORAL THEOLOGY IN LIVED THEOLOGY

Everyone belongs to the common priesthood, including ordained clergy. This equality applies likewise to lived theology. A critical look at the everyday lived theology of ordained and non-ordained people demonstrates that they are not so different. Within lived theology, the equality of various theological approaches and conceptions is programmatic.[16]

Much of what is supported by clergy in practice, on the Internet, and in church parishes, is grounded in their own experienced and lived theology. Thus preaching and pastoral action are always also shaped by one's personal lived theology. This is either in contrast to earlier personal experiences (as is often seen in the sharp dissociation from so-called evangelical or liberal approaches) or in

15. "In a You a person becomes an I" (Buber, *Das dialogische Prinzip*, 34).

16. In the discourse of contextual theology, the equality of various theologies has long been supported. Differences are justified by various contexts and life realities. Here difference is not regarded as a negative, but something to be encouraged: "Pluralism in theology, as well as on every level of Christian life, must not only be tolerated; it must be positively encouraged and cultivated" (Bevans, *Models of Contextual Theology*, 15).

their integration (but not necessarily reflection about them). Thus, in daily life, lived theologies are similar in that what is believed (contextual influence) and what "functions" is lived and preached.

But then what are the differences between lived theology and pastoral theology? The following discussion will briefly outline these differences, not in order to judge the two but to present their different functions.

Pastoral theology is also understood differently by various confessionally influenced academic traditions. In the Catholic understanding, pastoral theology refers to what Protestants call practical theology. Pastoral theology means "all dimensions and areas of ecclesial action."[17]

When we speak of pastoral theology here, we draw on the Protestant understanding:

> Protestant pastoral theology can be understood as an academic reflection of the mission of the church in the specific aspect of pastoral ministry. It considers theologically the ministry conferred in ordination and the tasks, obligations, and rights that emerge from this ministry as well as personal qualification for the office of preaching the gospel are described critically. It is reflection on profession—the profession and professionalism of the minister—with regard to the specific obligations they must attend to in the given ecclesial and societal circumstances.[18]

There is no unified understanding of what pastoral theology means. Likewise, there is no lived theology in the singular. Both pastoral theology and lived theology are diverse and multifaceted.

The main difference between the two forms of theology lies in the origin of the learning process. Lived theology is an experienced and embodied practice, which in turn seeks an outlet for expression. It is inductive, often implicit, and is not legitimized by academic study but must prove itself to be life-serving in life itself.

17. Fürst and Merkel, "Pastoraltheologie," 70.
18. Fürst and Merkel, "Pastoraltheologie," 76.

In contrast, pastoral theology is reflected upon academically and is learned through study (and in the best case connected with life and experience). Pastoral theology is connected with hermeneutical processes of reflection that are learned and practiced in academic education. In addition it contains many deductive and normative elements. In simplified terms, one could see pastoral theology as theory and lived theology as praxis.

Furthermore, the self-understanding of pastoral theology is different. The doctrine of the office of clergy is grounded in a vocational understanding: academically educated theologians are theological specialists. They often possess a professional identity and deep knowledge of their subject. In addition, for many clergy members, ordination brings a high degree of self-commitment.

In contrast, volunteers in parishes do not feel like experts and often do not understand the academic language of pastoral theology. They also generally do not see themselves from the perspective of the common priesthood and therefore only rarely lay claim to theological competence. Thus clergy possess and maintain the primary responsibility for theology. There are also significant differences in the understanding of the Bible. Clergy members are trained to approach the Bible critically. In addition, pastoral theology takes place on a meta-level (i.e., thinking about theology). Lived theology poses questions drawn from the concrete challenges of life. The dimensions of knowledge likewise differ: academically trained theologians possess a great deal of theoretical, religious, historical, and psychological general knowledge. This knowledge is not always connected with praxis and people's lived reality. Thus professionals run the risk of not being understood by other people and remain in an ivory tower. The theological knowledge that comes from the common priesthood is practical knowledge derived from daily experiences and becomes lived theology inductively.

These differences in theological conceptions must be taken into account. But if lived theology and pastoral theology are not pitted against one another and evaluated as such, but rather examined with regard to their functions and aims, the respective tasks of the different theologies emerge.

For this reason, the aim of a good academic practical theology cannot be to promote a dissociated treatment of students' personal experience and theological reflection. Reflective practical theology that takes lived theology into view enables students and future pastors to perceive, articulate, and reflect on personal and foreign religious experiences. Especially in a religiously individualized and pluralistic world, this ability is essential for theologians.[19]

This educational task should be a necessary part of the requirements of academic practical theology. Alongside the well-founded reflection on its areas of praxis, practical theology should also enable students and future clergy to engage in good hermeneutic maieutics in people's lives: "Contextualization, therefore, is not something on the fringes of the theological enterprise. It is at the very centre of what it means to do theology in today's world. Contextualization, in other words, is a theological imperative."[20]

Criticism of an alienated academic theology that produces clergy who are dissociated from personal experience has been expressed, among others, by Astley:

> I have argued before that only some of what goes on in university departments in England involves doing Christian theology, in the sense of the critical and reflective articulation, development and defense of Christian beliefs. And the extent to which that activity is truly religious theology that keeps closely in contact with the heart of Christian spirituality is an open question.[21]

Thus pastoral theology in fact has at its core the goal of perceiving, reflecting on, and supporting people's personal lived

19. "This correction consists in satisfying the demand that a theology as a professional theory of lived religion must not understand itself and operate as being in competition with non-professional interpretations of life within the lifeworld, but rather as a theoretical and practical support for them" (Pfleiderer, "'Gelebte Religion,'" 31).

20. Bevans, *Models of Contextual Theology*, 15.

21. Astley, *Ordinary Theology*, 74.

theology: "We need, rather, to begin with the working: to look and see what works in practice, and then to reflect theologically on that. . . . The theologian takes a step aside, as it were, now standing beside him or herself, giving up the former identity, at least to a certain degree."[22] And this is in the sense of Socratic maieutics, not something theologically deduced. In this respect, Bevans goes so far as to characterize "ordinary men and women" as specialists in the hermeneutics of context-specific theology, who, however, must be made aware of this through dialogical support.[23]

Even if the lived theology of ordained and non-ordained people does not differ greatly in daily life, academically educated theologians nevertheless ought to acquire the ability to be self-critical with respect to influences, experiences, contexts, and a personal lived theology—in order that they might become midwives for the lived theology of others.[24]

22. Astley, *Ordinary Theology*, 74.

23. Bevans, *Models of Contextual Theology*, 16–18.

24. "But academic education also enables self-reflection and critique; a theological course of studies guards against discounting the boundaries of one's own conviction and knowledge of God" (Wagner-Rau et al., "Pastoral-theologie," 122).

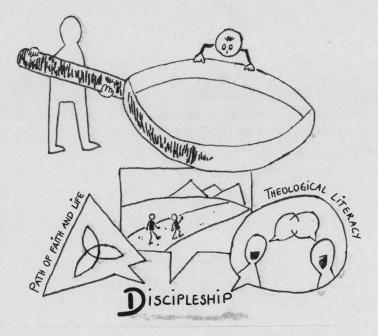

5

Toward a Pastoral Theology of Empowerment

In this closing chapter, six propositions offer a new impetus and open perspectives on a lived theology of the common priesthood for pastoral theology. This discussion will draw on the concept of maieutics.

PASTORAL THEOLOGY AS A MIDWIFE FOR LIVED THEOLOGY

To conceive of pastoral theology as maieutics, with the core task of empowering the common priesthood and supporting lived theology, is a paradigm shift leading away from approaches that emphasize the different nature of clergy and emphasize clergy as leading others to what is holy, the pastoral office as an office of remembrance or the perspective of professionalism.[1] In the quite varied pastoral-theological approaches discussed above, the ecclesial, ordained office is presented in different ways and various elements are emphasized. Thus the core tasks of pastoral theology are always

1. Cf. among others, Josuttis, *Die Einführung in das Leben*; Grözinger, *Die Kirche, ist sie noch zu retten?*; Karle, *Der Pfarrberuf als Profession.*

defined somewhat differently. Manfred Josuttis, for example, sees clergy as people who lead others into a holy zone that mediates spiritual techniques.[2] By contrast, Albrecht Grötzinger's image of the pastor is decidedly focused on the core task of intellectual achievement and the contextual and objectively correct mediation of biblical, Christian traditions in postmodern society.[3] Isolde Karle, in turn, supports the thesis that the position of pastor is to be understood as a profession that publicly represents the societally relevant field of religion.[4]

Despite the diversity of these approaches, they all share the fact that clergy are portrayed as having an advantage in knowledge and experience and taking on a function of generating and mediating content. The pastor is a specialist in church activities and theology.[5]

When the task of pastoral theology is considered in terms of its maieutic focus, the advantage in knowledge (which is not, however, an advantage in experience) only serves as a tool in the maieutic process.[6] The Socratic technique of maieutics[7] presupposes that one can only bring to light what is already present within a person. Within the horizon of the Christian understanding, this also includes the working of the spirit of God within a person, which must be discovered. For pastoral-theological maieutics, thorough and detailed listening and observation are indispensable.

---

2. Josuttis, *Die Einführung in das Leben*.

3. Grözinger, *Die Kirche, ist sie noch zu retten?*

4. Karle, *Der Pfarrberuf als Profession*.

5. This could be because specialized theological knowledge still serves a normative and authoritative function in church praxis.

6. This stands in contrast to concepts that seek to convey content and expertise deductively. Of course, Plato's Socrates is a person who actually already knows what ought to emerge from the conversation, and often enough the dialogue partner limits herself to a "yes, certainly" or "no, of course not." In these discussions, however, this aspect of Plato's Socrates is not the central focus, but rather his function as a midwife.

7. Whether Socrates in fact compared his philosophical work with midwifery is historically uncertain and only documented in Plato's texts.

In Plato's accounts, Socrates allows his conversation partners to uncover for themselves the truth of the matter under discussion but supports the process through apposite questioning. Thus the insight gained is "born" with the assistance of this midwifery technique.

The crucial aspect of the metaphor of the midwife is the attitude. A midwife can only ever carry out her work in a supportive role. This also applies to a pastoral theology of empowerment: "Theology must rather be an activity of dialogue, emerging out of a mutual respect between 'faith-ful' but not technically trained people and faith-ful and listening professionals."[8]

With regard to the aims of lived theology, academically educated theologians, together with all other people who theologize, are able to carry out everyday-theological hermeneutic processes and open up spaces for religious experience. This is a matter of "opening spaces of experience for people in which they can create hope beyond what they achieve themselves and thus are able to face their own uncertainty."[9] Thus it is a matter of marking and opening the subjective approaches to independent ways of living out one's faith. Everyone determines for themselves what form and what expression this takes.[10] The form of maieutics that pastoral theology can contribute is theological reflection and inductive hermeneutics. This is central: "It provides the key by which to apply the rigours of the academy to the swamp of messy, real-life situation. It converts the role of academic theology in ministry from dominating master to useful servant."[11] Pastoral theology can bring into play the "potential for stimulation," but it should nevertheless not seek to be a normative authority.

The same can be said of its rootedness, which also applies to public theology, namely, that lived theology "is able to legitimize an essential space of influence and creation for itself only if it engages as intensely as possible in analyzing present circumstances,

8. Bevans, *Models of Contextual Theology*, 18.

9. Grethlein, "Gemeindeentwicklung," 505.

10. H. Luther, *Religion und Alltag*, 13.

11. Heywood, "Educating Ministers of Character," 20.

but is at the same time, according to its own self-understanding, [guided by] theological groundwork that is as clear and distinct as possible."[12]

THE COLLABORATIVE DANCE—A METAPHOR FOR A RECIPROCAL LEARNING PROCESS

Lived theology is creative communication about God and life lived in God's presence. This can be compared to a dance floor to which a pastoral theology of empowerment offers an invitation and where lived theology and the pastoral theology of empowerment dance together.

Already in the 1980s, Charles Gerkin spoke of the "pastor as interpretative guide."[13] In this, Gerkin placed the focus on the reciprocal nature of this activity: "a relationship of mutual exploration and reflective consideration of options may be possible between pastor and people, facilitating greater freedom and honesty on both sides."[14]

A pastoral theology of empowerment moderates between people's concrete context and Christian tradition. It engages with people as a midwife in the process of searching and asks how the gospel is manifest today and in specific contexts. At the same time, it is always guided by biblical and Christian tradition in terms of their present relevance to life. The nature of the shared dance as interwoven and cooperative results in all sides learning from and being changed by one another.

COME AND SEE—DEVELOPING POTENTIAL

A pastoral theology of empowerment serves lived theology in that it helps the latter come to life. Supporting the communication of the gospel in this context means strengthening the common

12. Schlag, *Öffentliche Kirche*, 17.

13. Gerkin, *Introduction to Pastoral Care*, 113–14.

14. Gerkin, *Widening the Horizons*, 99.

priesthood's theological literacy and capacity for expression, thus creating a public space for lived theology in digital and analog society.

In this, pastoral theology is challenged to the following:

> The pastoral guide does not take people on the same old trip but travels with them into new territory. Together, they must learn the lay of the land and the path available to them. This is a collaborative activity. The guide must attend carefully to the resources of the travelers and the particular journey they hope to take, as well as contributing her own expertise.[15]

This form of pastoral theology deals with the world of experience of specific people's lived theology. It is therefore relational and strives to create a non-hierarchical, dialogical level of communication. It encounters the phenomenon of lived theology on equal footing. As is the case in Socratic maieutics, a pastoral theology of empowerment intuits what has not yet come to light, the theological potential, that which has yet to be born. It supports people in developing their own lived theology and articulating it collaboratively and in social networks. That is, it actively promotes and engages with the development of a lived theology of the common priesthood.

FUNDAMENTAL ATTITUDE—DIALOGUE AND RESONANCE

The primary attitude of a pastoral theology of empowerment is dialogical.[16] This mindset is not primarily a matter of conversational

15. Osmer, *Practical Theology*, 19–20.

16. Grethlein has pointed out that "today the pastoral perspective of practical-theological work [must be] reoriented. It is apparent that the functions of indoctrination and—long taken as self-evident—(authoritarian) reprimanding by the 'ecclesial office' are losing significance. They are transformed in communicative, moderating tasks which are concerned with conveying concrete life situations and Christian stimuli. In theological diction, the common priesthood of all baptised Christians (WA 6.564) or, in religio-sociological terms, the religious productivity of people today changes

technique, but rather an "attitude toward dealing with oneself and one's own personal truths, toward dealing with other people their personal truths."[17] Thus the fundamental dialogical attitude is not attached to a course of conversation, but rather takes place continuously within hermeneutical processes of communication, in relationships, in narrative-biographical activities, in religious practices, in semiotic actions and interpretations. Dialogue as an attitude and tool of pastoral theology is directed toward the common priesthood and "does not intend to coopt . . . but rather to perceive and take seriously its abilities, aspirations, reflective needs for orientation, and—most importantly—its competence."[18]

The fundamental dialogical attitude in a pastoral theology aims at empowering the common priesthood and ought to support both individual theological responsibility and communal aspects of lived theology.

A helpful model for thinking about this process is that of resonance. Together, lived theology and a pastoral theology of empowerment create a relationship of resonance[19] with that which necessarily and existentially concerns the individual, with the "ultimate concern" in Tillich's words.[20] In this resonant space lived theology can be considered and expanded, and be expressed. Insights from children's and youth theology can also provide an impetus for inductive processes of development like those of lived theology. The substance of these theologies are tested and experienced: "Traditional interpretations can only be meaningful

---

the meaning and the task of pastoral activity. In short, into the place of teachers and guardians of faith, the communicator or communication of the gospel has stepped, which must first carefully perceive and understand the situation of the conversation partner. Practical theology thus becomes a theory of communicating the gospel in the present, in which pastors have an important task, which, however, can only be fulfilled together with others" (Grethlein, *Praktische Theologie*, 5).

17. Benesch, *Psychologie des Dialogs*, 11.

18. Müller, "Bedingungen eines gelingenden theologischen Diskurses," 167.

19. Rosa, *Resonanz*, 435–36.

20. Tillich, *Dynamics of Faith*, 110.

if they are explored and tested in thoughts and actions. Creating a space for this is the purpose of every subject-oriented religious didactics."[21] The normativity of meaning and experience is not simply taught, but constructed individually and personally, developed further on the basis of new experiences, and must prove itself in daily lived existence.[22]

FROM PRIVATE EXPERIENCE TO PUBLIC ACTION

A pastoral theology of empowerment contributes to this in that it enables lived theology to unfold in church and society, in digital and analog form, because it is based on the conviction that even today the Christian agenda and lived theology promote life and serve life.

Lived theology is thus also a form of mission theology. Not in a colonial-paternalistic form, but one which must prove to be helpful and life-serving in the concrete context of life. Especially in connection with the public nature of lived theology, the following should be taken into account: "Here it should be remembered that the crucial, publicly impactful spread of the early Christian faith took place crucially through so-called laypersons, with their private and professional contacts, in the midst of everyday life in the sense of a microcommunication in small, private, and semi-public settings."[23]

The common priesthood is thus freed from its apprehensive marginality and impacts the concrete communication of the gospel.

In the digital realm, this small, sometimes unremarkable microcommunication can be seen in many areas. For this very reason its public impact should not be underestimated. With hashtags like #dnkgtt, #prayfor, #twomplet, #twaudes, #SlatePrays, #SlateSpeak, etc., lively discourses of lived theology and periods of shared

21. Kammeyer, "Kindheitsforschung und Kindertheologie," 11.

22. This process is described by Arnett as "to think for themselves with regard to religious issues" umschrieben. Arnett, *Emerging Adulthood*, 212–14.

23. Schlag, *Öffentliche Kirche*, 28.

spirituality take place on a daily basis. Thus, for example, the hashtag #twomplet was created on January 14th, 2014, by Benedikt Johannes Heider (born 1995). The then-nineteen-year-old was a high school graduate who now studies theology and came up with the idea of creating the hashtag #twomplet from "Twitter" and "Komplet" (German for "compline").

Since the founding of this Twitter prayer, there has been an evening prayer by the @twomplet account almost daily. @twomplet has 2,167 followers, half of whom are active participants, and there are more than thirty prayer leaders. The prayer takes place every evening at 9:00 p.m. and can be prayed while at home, traveling, in the train, or in the office. Since the tweets remain visible, it is also possible to pray at a later time.

The account is ecumenical and thus the prayer takes on slightly different forms depending on who leads it. The evening prayer is based on the compline from the Liturgy of the Hours, but the prayer leaders bring in their own traditions and ideas. People from Protestant (Lutheran, Reformed, Uniate), Catholic, Old Catholic, Baptist, and non-denominational traditions are represented. Those who join in the prayer participate with likes, retweets, and by sharing their own prayer requests during the intercessory prayer. Especially during crises and attacks, people find comfort and support in such digital spaces. For example, on the evening following the attacks in Paris on November 13, 2015, the hashtag #twomplet was used in eighty tweets with 44,000 views, with up to 6,000 views per tweet and 650 likes.

These microcommunications and their impacts ought to be analyzed and considered more intensely from practical theological, as well as missiological, perspectives.

Kirchehoch2 and Homebrewed Christianity were examples of digital lived theology, theological productivity, and its impact. The pastoral theological dimension is inherent in these examples because it is theologians who create the resonant space or who log in to the discussions of lived theology. In these examples, the church and individuals were successful in becoming part of a meaningful public discourse of lived theology. This was not done in a normative way, but rather by using broad and clear theological frameworks.

In Kirchehoch2, theologians were granted pastoral-theological freedom to discuss Christian tradition in creative processes in the digital context and to participate in digital discourses. The gifts and interests of female theologians were interwoven with their mission.

In the parish context as well, it is the microcommunication of the lived theology of the common priesthood that leads to change. Here I propose that church communities with the ability to articulate themselves are also vibrant communities. These are churches whose priesthood is capable of bearing witness to life and to faith. In this, an adequate social organization of Christians today is fundamental.[24] However, this can vary greatly depending on context, lifeworld, and virtuality. There is always also a prophetic dimension inherent to ordained ministry, particularly in situations where theological, political, ethical, and structural conceptions hinder and constrict life, as well as where ecclesial administration, dogmatism, and bureaucracy get in the way of the common priesthood discovering and developing lived theology.

A PASTORAL THEOLOGY OF EMPOWERMENT REQUIRES THAT ORDAINED MINISTRY HAVE CREATIVE FREEDOM

In concluding we must once again point to the role of ministerial personnel. Current developments in pastoral ministry call into question the core tasks formulated here of empowering the common priesthood and its lived theology. The overwhelming demands made of a profession in the humanities for achievement and competency due to organizational development suffocate the creative hermeneutic processes of lived theology. Thus ministers lack the necessary and independent space for thought and freedom.

24. Grethlein, "Gemeindeentwicklung," 495.

Interpreting the gospel in a way that is relevant to people's lives—in digital and analog form—should remain the core of ministerial and theological work. This free, relational, intellectual activity must be enabled and promoted at an institutional level.

Ministers ought to be able to pursue their core task without being coopted by structural demands and supply-led activism. Instead, their ordination ought to form the guiding framework of their ministerial activity. The challenge of pastoral theology is to recognize, accommodate, discuss, and promote concrete movements of searching and initial impulses within and beyond the parish, in digital and analog form. In this, one must not overlook the implicit mission at soup kitchens, the volunteer carpenters who renovate church community buildings, the participants in finance or property committees, the mourning widow who engages in pastoral counseling, the countless little hashtags, digital mourning groups, online prayer platforms, etc. These are also searching movements of lived theology guided by discipleship.

A pastoral theology of empowerment requires time and space for these processes. It must be able to listen and observe in order to fearlessly join in the public discourse of lived theology and simultaneously promote this discourse in the church and in society.

Ultimately, though, such a pastoral theology must not forget that it is not the controlling authority. The level of explicit and public commitment varies—we may remember here the Ethiopian of Acts, who went on his way full of joy and only later began to preach.[25]

Lived theology is a public commodity, an expression of the realization of the common priesthood. In this it is neither the property of privatization that operates on organizational logic and university criticism, nor can it be claimed and coopted by authoritarian bodies like the church and university.

Ecclesial praxis and university practical theology come together in that they both, from different perspectives, are oriented toward the promotion, reflection, and maieutics of lived theology.

25. Cf. Acts 8:26–40.

A Personal Afterword—
Fragments of a Sermon

It is not only my practical-theological conviction, but also my personal conviction, that the agenda of the common priesthood and its lived theology are foundational for practical theology, pastoral theology, and for church-theoretical thinking. The concern here is that people who have not studied theology be perceived and taken seriously as representatives of lived theology, in order for them to be able to become a constitutive part of ecclesial and theological praxis. For in lived theology, the life relevance of the gospel is expressed plurally, openly, multifacetedly, and sometimes also controversially.

Lived theology is not only based in experience, it is also itself an experience that changes a person at the core of their identity. In this sense, it is not simply a sum of experiences, but a change of the self and its system of meaning that brings the entirety of the past, present, and future into God's presence. Life can thus be interpreted in a new light: a person is God's creation, living in the presence of God. One does not create this understanding oneself; rather, it happens to a person and requires freedom and time to take form and find expression.

Lived theology is the theology that is experienced and lived. It is the theology that is part of everyday life, that participates in the high points of life and helps to interpret life and set it in a new light. But it is also the theology that is still there in the deepest darkness, in depression and loneliness, and is greater than doubt.

Perhaps it is the stubbornness and tenacity that shines a light in the darkness (John 1:5), even when one does not feel or see it. It is often available in the depths of life in lament and doubt and is like a promise: all these emotions, one's own darkness or happiness—they do not have the last word. Behind what is perceptible to and doable by humanity, a shift in perspective takes place that is supportive of life.

Lived theology is the theology that must prove to support and serve life in everyday existence. It is constantly changed a little by experiences and given a new interpretation by life. At the same time, life is repeatedly reinterpreted by lived theology. Lived theology remains in need of interpretation in daily life, comparable to a movement of searching for expression, speech, and resonance. It becomes visible only in lived life.

This must always be understood as relational; it requires a conversation partner, in digital or analog space. Lived theology requires encouragement for visibility and it needs the hermeneutical companionship of other priests and, ideally, of a pastoral theology of empowerment. Independent theological productivity then becomes visible in this relational resonant space: through contemplation, questioning, reframing, comfort, and prayer.

This lived theology is a searching discipleship and requires searching companionship, not know-it-all indoctrination.

Bibliography

"175.1—Kirchenordnung der evangelisch-reformierten Kirche des Kantons St. Gallen." https://www.gesetzessammlung.sg.ch/app/de/texts_of_law/175.1.

"About." https://trippfuller.com/about/.

Arendt, Hannah. *Vita activa oder Vom tätigen Leben.* 3rd ed. Munich: Piper, 2005.

Armstrong, Michael R. "Some Ordinary Theology of Assisted Dying." *Ecclesial Practices* 5 (2018) 39–53.

Arnett, Jeffrey Jensen. *Emerging Adulthood: The Winding Road from the Late Teens through the Twenties.* 2nd ed. Oxford: Oxford University Press, 2014.

Asmussen, Hans. *Das Priestertum aller Gläubigen.* Stuttgart: Quell-Verlag, 1946.

Astley, Jeff. "The Analysis, Investigation and Application of Ordinary Theology." In *Exploring Ordinary Theology: Everyday Christian Believing and the Church*, edited by Leslie J. Francis and Jeff Astley, 1–9. Farnham, UK: Ashgate, 2013.

———. *Ordinary Theology: Looking, Listening and Learning in Theology.* Farnham, UK: Ashgate, 2002.

"Barmer Theologische Erklärung." https://www.ekd.de/Barmer-Theologische-Erklarung-Thesen-11296.html.

Barth, Hans-Martin. *Einander Priester sein: Allgemeines Priestertum in ökumenischer Perspektive.* Göttingen: Vandenhoeck & Ruprecht, 1990.

Bauman, Zygmunt. *Flaneure, Spieler und Touristen: Essays zu postmodernen Lebensformen.* 1st ed. Hamburg: Hamburger, 2006.

Beck, Ulrich. "Jenseits von Stand und Klasse? Soziale Ungleichheiten, gesellschaftliche Individualisierungsprozesse und die Entstehung neuer sozialer Formationen und Identitäten." In *Soziale Ungleichheiten*, edited by Reinhard Kreckel, 35–74. Soziale Welt; Sonderband 2. Göttingen: Schwartz, 1983.

Benesch, Michael. *Psychologie des Dialogs.* Vienna: UTB, 2011.

Berger, Peter L. *The Many Altars of Modernity: Toward a Paradigm for Religion in a Pluralist Age.* Berlin: de Gruyter, 2014.

Bevans, Stephen B. *Models of Contextual Theology*. Maryknoll, NY: Orbis, 2002.

Bils, Sandra. "Kirche2—Eine ökumenische Bewegung." In *Fresh X—Frisch. Neu. Innovativ: Und es ist Kirche*, edited by Hans-Hermann Pompe et al., 50–56. Neukirchen-Vluyn: Neukirchener Aussaat, 2016.

"Bischof: Kirche muss sich auf weniger Pastoren vorbereiten." https://www. nordkirche.de/nachrichten/nachrichten-detail/nachricht/bischof-kirche-muss-sich-auf-weniger-pastoren-vorbereiten/.

Bonhoeffer, Dietrich. *Nachfolge*. Edited by Martin Kuske and Ilse Tödt. 3rd ed. Dietrich Bonhoeffer Werke 4. Gütersloh: Kaiser, 2002.

———. "Wer bin ich." https://www.dietrich-bonhoeffer.net/predigttext/wer-bin-ich/.

Bordieu, Pierre. "Ökonomisches Kapital—Kulturelles Kapital—Soziales Kapital." In *Soziale Ungleichheiten*, edited by Reinhard Kreckel, 183–98. Soziale Welt; Sonderband 2. Göttingen: Schwartz, 1983.

Bowman, Donna. *The Homebrewed Christianity Guide to Being Human: Becoming the Best Bag of Bones You Can Be*. Minneapolis: Fortress, 2018.

Browning, Don. *Fundamental Practical Theology: Descriptive and Strategic Proposals*. Minneapolis: Fortress, 1996.

Buber, Martin. *Das dialogische Prinzip: Ich und Du; Zwiesprache; Die Frage an den Einzelnen; Elemente des Zwischenmenschlichen; Zur Geschichte des dialogischen Prinzips*. 17th ed. Gütersloh: Gütersloher, 2017.

Bundeszentrale für politische Bildung. "Empowerment-Landkarte: Diskurse, normative Rahmung, Kritik." www.bpb.de/apuz/180866/empowerment-landkarte.

Campbell, Heidi A., and Stephen Garner. *Networked Theology: Negotiating Faith in Digital Culture*. Grand Rapids: Baker Academic, 2016.

Cobb, John, and David Griffin. *Process Theology: An Introductory Exposition*. Rev. ed. Philadelphia: Westminster, 1976.

Coenen-Marx, Cornelia, and Beate Hofmann, eds. *Symphonie—Drama—Powerplay: Zum Zusammenspiel von Haupt- und Ehrenamt in der Kirche*. Stuttgart: Kohlhammer, 2017.

Consalvo, Mia, and Charles Ess. "Introduction." In *The Handbook of Internet Studies*, edited by Mia Consalvo and Charles Ess, 1–8. 1st ed. Malden, MA: Wiley-Blackwell 2012.

Cray, Graham, et al. *Mission-Shaped Church: Church Planting and Fresh Expressions of Church in a Changing Context*. London: Church House, 2004.

DFG-Projekt. "Gelebte Theologie." https://www.uni-saarland.de/fachrichtung/kath-theologie/projekte/dfg-projekt-gelebte-theologie.html.

Digitale Bibliothek 012. *RGG Religion in Geschichte und Gegenwart*. 3rd ed. Tübingen: Mohr Siebeck, 2004.

Dinter, Astrid, et al., eds. *Einführung in die Empirische Theologie: Gelebte Religion erforschen*. Göttingen: UTB, 2007.

Elias, Norbert. *Über den Prozess der Zivilisation: Soziogenetische und psychogenetische Untersuchungen*. Vol. 1, *Wandlungen des Verhaltens in den weltlichen Oberschichten des Abendlandes.* 30th ed. Frankfurt am Main: Suhrkamp, 2010.

"Engagiert im Ehrenamt." https://www.nordkirche.de/dazugehoeren/im-ehrenamt/.

Failing, Wolf-Eckart, and Hans-Günter Heimbrock. *Gelebte Religion wahrnehmen: Lebenswelt—Alltagskultur—Religionspraxis.* Stuttgart: Kohlhammer, 1998.

Federal Office for Statistics. "Freiwilligenarbeit." https://www.bfs.admin.ch/bfs/de/home/statistiken/arbeit-erwerb/unbezahlte-arbeit/freiwilligenarbeit.html.

Francis, Leslie J., and Jeff Astley, eds. *Exploring Ordinary Theology: Everyday Christian Believing and the Church.* Farnham, UK: Ashgate, 2013.

"Freiwillige machen die Kirche glaubwürdig." https://www.kathluzern.ch/engagement/freiwillig-im-einsatz.html.

"Freiwilligenarbeit." https://www.kirchenbund.ch/de/themen/freiwilligenarbeit.

"Freiwilligenarbeit—ein Gewinn für alle." https://www.ref-sg.ch/freiwilligenarbeit.html.

"Freiwilligenmonitor." https://sgg-ssup.ch/de/freiwilligenmonitor.html.

Friedli, Richard, et al. "Priestertum." In *Religion in Geschichte und Gegenwart Online,* edited by Hans Dieter Betz et al. 4th ed. Tübingen: Mohr Siebeck, 2004. https://referenceworks.brillonline.com/entries/religion-in-geschichte-und-gegenwart/*-COM_024468.

Fürst, Walter, and Friedemann Merkel. "Pastoraltheologie." In *Theologische Realenzyklopädie Online,* edited by Horst Robert Balz and Wilfried Härle. Berlin: de Gruyter, 1996. https://db.degruyter.com/view/TRE/TRE.26_070_32?pi=0&moduleId=common-word-wheel&dbJumpTo=Pastoraltheologie.

Gerkin, Charles V. *An Introduction to Pastoral Care.* Nashville: Abingdon, 1997.

———. *Widening the Horizons: Pastoral Responses to a Fragmented Society.* Philadelphia: Westminster, 1986.

Goffman, Erving. *Stigma: Über Techniken der Bewältigung beschädigter Identität.* Translated by Frigga Haug. Frankfurt am Main: Suhrkamp, 2010.

Gräb, Wilhelm. *Religion als Deutung des Lebens: Perspektiven einer Praktischen Theologie gelebter Religion.* Gütersloh: Gütersloher, 2006.

Green, Laurie. *Let's Do Theology: Resources for Contextual Theology.* 2nd ed. London: Mowbray, 2009.

Grethlein, Christian. "Gemeindeentwicklung. Gemeindeaufbau/church growth/Gemeindeleben/Verein." In *Handbuch Praktische Theologie,* edited by Wilhelm Gräb and Birgit Weyel, 495–506. 1st ed. Gütersloh: Gütersloher, 2007.

———. *Praktische Theologie.* Berlin: de Gruyter, 2012.

Grözinger, Albrecht. *Die Kirche, ist sie noch zu retten?* Gütersloh: Gütersloher, 1998.

Grözinger, Albrecht, and Georg Pfleiderer, eds. *"Gelebte Religion" als Programmbegriff Systematischer und Praktischer Theologie.* Zürich: Theologischer Verlag Zürich, 2002.

Grümme, Bernhard. *Aufbruch in die Öffentlichkeit? Reflexionen zum "public turn" in der Religionspädagogik.* 1st ed. Bielefeld, Germany: Transcript Verlag, 2018.

Härle, Wilfried. *Dogmatik.* 3rd ed. Berlin: de Gruyter, 2007.

Härle, Wilfried, and Harald Goertz. "Priester/Priestertum." In *Theologische Realenzyklopädie Online*, edited by Wassilios Klein et al., 27:402–10. Berlin: de Gruyter, 1997.

Härle, Wilfried, et al. *Wachsen gegen den Trend: Analysen von Gemeinden, mit denen es aufwärts geht.* 4th unaltered ed. Leipzig: Evangelische Verlagsanstalt, 2012.

Hermelink, Jan. *Kirchliche Organisation und das Jenseits des Glaubens: Eine praktisch-theologische Theorie der evangelischen Kirche.* Gütersloh: Gütersloher, 2011.

Herriger, Norbert. *Empowerment in der Sozialen Arbeit: Eine Einführung.* 5th ed. Stuttgart: Kohlhammer, 2014.

Herrmann, Maria, and Sandra Bils, eds. *Vom Wandern und Wundern: Fremdsein und prophetische Ungeduld in der Kirche.* Würzburg: Echter, 2017.

Heywood, David. "Educating Ministers of Character." *Journal of Adult Theological Education* 10 (2013) 4–24.

Hofmann, Beate. "Ehrenamt und Freiwilligkeit." In *Handbuch für Kirchen- und Gemeindeentwicklung*, edited by Ralph Kunz and Thomas Schlag, 140–50. 1st ed. Neukirchen-Vluyn: Neukirchener Theologie, 2014.

Hoover, Stewart M. "Religious Authority in the Media Age." In *The Media and Religious Authority*, edited by Stewart M. Hoover, 15–36. University Park: Pennsylvania State University Press, 2016.

Impulse Paper of the Council of the EKD. "Kirche der Freiheit." https://www.ekd.de/ekd_de/ds_doc/kirche-der-freiheit.pdf.

Jakob, Samuel. "Reformierte Gemeindeleitung—Das Zürcher 'Zuordnungsmodell.'" In *Schweizerisches Jahrbuch für Kirchenrecht*, edited by Dieter Kraus et al., 47–62. Bern: Lang, 2014.

James, William. *The Varieties of Religious Experience.* 1902. Reprint, Scotts Valley, CA: CreateSpace, 2013.

Josuttis, Manfred. *Die Einführung in das Leben: Pastoraltheologie zwischen Phänomenologie und Spiritualität.* Gütersloh: Kaiser, Gütersloher, 1996.

Junge, Matthias, and Thomas Kron. *Zygmunt Bauman: Soziologie zwischen Postmoderne, Ethik und Gegenwartsdiagnose.* 3rd ed. Wiesbaden: VS Verlag für Sozialwissenschaften, 2014.

Kammeyer, Katharina. "Kindheitsforschung und Kindertheologie: Ein kindertheologischer Blick auf Beiträge soziologischer Kindheitsforschung." *Theo-web: Zeitschrift für Religionspädagogik* 11.2 (2012) 38–63. www.theo-web.de/zeitschrift/ausgabe-2012-01/05.pdf.

Karle, Isolde. *Der Pfarrberuf als Profession: Eine Berufstheorie im Kontext der modernen Gesellschaft.* 3rd ed. Stuttgart: Kreuz, 2011.

"Kirchehochzwei." https://www.evangelisch.de/blogs/kreuz-queer/142329/ 23-02-2017.

"Kirchenordnung der evangelisch-reformierten Kirche des Kantons St. Gallen." https://www.ref-sg.ch/files/content/dokumente-pdf/gueltige_ erlasse/10/11_20_kirchenordnung_der_evangelisch_reformierten_ kirche_des_kantons_st_gallen.pdf.

Klie, Thomas. "Kasualgemeinde." In *Handbuch für Kirchen- und Gemeindeentwicklung,* edited by Ralph Kunz and Thomas Schlag, 281–87. 1st ed. Neukirchen-Vluyn: Neukirchener Theologie, 2014.

Koch, Muriel, and Thomas Schlag. "Results from Switzerland." In *Confirmation, Faith, and Volunteerism: A Longitudinal Study on Protestant Adolescents in the Transition towards Adulthood; European Perspectives,* edited by Friedrich Schweitzer et al., 151–61. Gütersloh: Gütersloher, 2017.

Kunz, Ralph. "Zur Notwendigkeit einer Theologie des Laientums und zu den Chancen und Stolpersteinen der gemeinsamen Verantwortung in Gemeinde und Kirche." In *Alle sind gefragt: Priestertum aller Gläubigen heute,* edited by Ralph Kunz and Matthias Zeindler, 29–52. Zürich: Theologischer Verlag Zürich 2018.

Kunz, Ralph, and Matthias Zeindler, eds. *Alle sind gefragt: Priestertum aller Gläubigen heute.* Zürich: Theologischer Verlag Zürich, 2018.

Kunz, Ralph, and Thomas Schlag. "Gemeindeautonomie und Zuordnungs- modell in reformierter Perspektive: Kirchentheoretische Orientierungen und Folgerungen für die kirchenleitende Praxis." In *Schweizerisches Jahrbuch für Kirchenrecht,* edited by Dieter Kraus, 71–117. Bern: Lang, 2018.

Lange, Ernst. *Sprachschule für die Freiheit: Bildung als Problem und Funktion der Kirche.* München: Kaiser, 1980.

Leitfaden Freiwilligenarbeit: "Leitfaden zur Freiwilligenarbeit für reformierte Kirchgemeinden." https://www.refbejuso.ch/fileadmin/user_upload/Down- loads/Gemeindedienste_und_Bildung/Freiwilligenarbeit/Materialien/1803_ leitfaden-freiwilligenarbeit_alles.pdf.

Leonard, Bill. *The Homebrewed Christianity Guide to Church History: Flaming Heretics and Heavy Drinkers.* Minneapolis: Fortress, 2017.

Little, Brian. *Mein Ich, die anderen und wir: Die Psychologie der Persönlichkeit und die Kunst des Wohlbefindens.* Translated by Martina Wiese. Berlin: Springer Spektrum, 2015.

Luckmann, Thomas. *Die unsichtbare Religion.* Edited by Hubert Knoblauch. 8th ed. Frankfurt am Main: Suhrkamp, 1991.

Luther, Henning. *Religion und Alltag: Bausteine zu einer Praktischen Theologie des Subjekts.* Stuttgart: Radius, 1992.

Luther, Martin. *D. Martin Luthers Werke* (WA). Vol. 40/2, 2. *Galatervorlesung (cap. 5–6) 1531; Vorlesungen über Psalm 2, 45 und 51.* N.p.: Böhlaus, 1532.

Meyer, Joyce. "Wie man Gottes Reden hört." *AUFATMEN: Das Magazin zum Gott begegnen und authentisch leben.* https://scm-bundes-verlag.ch/medien/lesen/aufatmen.

———. *Wie man Gottes Reden hört: Erkennen Sie Gottes Stimme und treffen Sie die richtigen Entscheidungen.* 3rd ed. Hamburg: Joyce Meyer Ministries, 2015.

Mildenberger, Friedrich. *Biblische Dogmatik: Eine biblische Theologie in dogmatischer Perspektive.* Stuttgart: Kohlhammer, 1991.

Moynagh, Michael. *Church for Every Context: An Introduction to Theology and Practice.* London: SCM, 2012.

Müller, Sabrina. "Bedingungen eines gelingenden theologischen Diskurses mit jungen Freiwilligen." In *Jahrbuch für Jugendtheologie: "Jedes Mal in der Kirche kam ich zum Nachdenken": Jugendliche und Kirche,* edited by Thomas Schlag and Bert Roebben, 4:160–70. Stuttgart: Calwer, 2016.

———. "Discipleship—Eine kirchentheoretische Grundfigur in der Spannung von Bekenntnisorientierung und Deutungsoffenheit." *Praktische Theologie* 53 (2018) 34–37.

———. *Fresh Expressions of Church: Ekklesioligische Beobachtungen und Interpretationen einer neuen kirchlichen Bewegung.* Zürich: Theologischer Verlag Zürich, 2016.

———. "How Ordinary Moments Become Religious Experiences: A Process-Related Practical Theological Perspective." In *Religious Experience and Experiencing Religion in Religious Education,* edited by Ulrich Riegel et al., 79–96. Münster: Waxmann, 2018.

Oerter, Rolf, and Leo Montada. *Entwicklungspsychologie.* 5th ed. Weinheim: Beltz PVU, 2002.

Osmer, Richard R. *Practical Theology: An Introduction.* Grand Rapids: Eerdmans, 2008.

Pfleiderer, Georg. "'Gelebte Religion'—Notizen zu einem Theoriephänomen." In *"Gelebte Religion" als Programmbegriff Systematischer und Praktischer Theologie,* edited by Albrecht Grözinger and Georg Pfleiderer, 23–42. Zürich: Theologischer Verlag Zürich, 2002.

Pinsky, Mark I. *The Gospel According to the Simpsons: Bigger and Possibly Even Better!* Expanded ed. Louisville: Westminster John Knox, 2007.

Rappaport, Julian. "In Praise of Paradox: A Social Policy of Empowerment over Prevention." *American Journal of Community Psychology* 9 (1981) 1–25.

———. *Studies in Empowerment: Steps toward Understanding and Action.* New York: Routledge, 1984.

Recke, Martin. "Wundersames Wanderbuch." https://medium.com/@mr94/wundersames-wanderbuch-bff3ae51bee8.

"Related Churches | HTB Church." www.htb.org.uk/about-htb/related-churches.

Ricoeur, Paul. *Der Konflikt der Interpretationen: Ausgewählte Aufsätze.* Edited by Daniel Creutz and Hans-Helmuth Gander. Freiburg: Karl Alber, 2010.

Rosa, Hartmut. *Resonanz: Eine Soziologie der Weltbeziehung*. 5th ed. Berlin: Suhrkamp, 2016.

Salazar, Carles. "Believing Minds: Steps to an Ecology of Religious Ideas." In *Religious Experience and Experiencing Religion in Religious Education*, edited by Ulrich Riegel et al., 23–42. 1st ed. Münster: Waxmann, 2018.

Sallmann, Martin. "Das allgemeine Priestertum in kirchengeschichtlicher Perspektive." In *Alle sind gefragt: Priestertum aller Gläubigen heute*, edited by Ralph Kunz and Matthias Zeindler, 53–63. Zürich: Theologischer Verlag Zürich, 2018.

Schlag, Thomas. *Öffentliche Kirche: Grunddimensionen einer praktisch-theologischen Kirchentheorie*. Zürich: Theologischer Verlag Zürich, 2012.

———. "Öffentlichkeit 4.0." In *Reflektierte Kirche: Beiträge zur Kirchentheorie*, edited by Konrad Merzyn et al., 321–36. 1st ed. Leipzig: Evangelische Verlagsanstalt, 2018.

Schleiermacher, Friedrich. *On Religion: Speeches to Its Cultured Despisers*. Translated by John Oman. London: Kegan Paul, Trench, Trübner, 1893.

———. *Über die Religion*: Reden an die Gebildeten unter ihren Verächtern (1799). In *Kritische Gesamtausgabe: Schriften aus der Berliner Zeit 1769–1799*, edited by Günter Meckenstock, 1.2:185–326. Berlin: de Gruyter, 1984.

Schliesser, Benjamin. "Reforamtion als Resonanz. Kontinuität und Wandel in neutestamentlicher Perspektive." In Kirche(n)gestalten. Re-Formation von Kirche und Gemeinde in Zeiten des Umbruchs, edited by Kolja Koeniger and Jens Monsees, 55–76. Göttingen: Vandenhoeck & Ruprecht, 2019.

Schweitzer, Friedrich. "Bildung." In *Handbuch für Kirchen- und Gemeindeentwicklung*, edited by Ralph Kunz and Thomas Schlag, 253–60. 1st ed. Neukirchen-Vluyn: Neukirchener Theologie, 2014.

Schweizerischer Evangelischer Kirchenbund (SEK). "Kulturelle Wirkungen der Reformation am Beispiel der Schweiz." https://www.ref-500.ch/sites/default/files/media/PDF/wort_bild/reformation_im_kontext.pdf.

Simonson, Julia, ed. *Freiwilliges Engagement in Deutschland: Der Deutsche Freiwilligensurvey 2014*. Wiesbaden: Springer Fachmedien Wiesbaden, 2017.

Stenger, Mary Ann. "Faith (and Religion)." In *The Cambridge Companion to Paul Tillich*, edited by Russell Re Manning, 91–104. Cambridge: Cambridge University Press, 2009.

Streib, Heinz, and Carsten Gennerich. *Jugend und Religion: Bestandsaufnahmen, Analysen und Fallstudien zur Religiosität Jugendlicher*. Weinheim, Germany: Beltz Juventa, 2011.

Taves, Ann. "Finding and Articulating Meaning in Secular Experience." In *Religious Experience and Experiencing Religion in Religious Education*, edited by Ulrich Riegel et al., 13–22. 1st ed. Münster: Waxmann, 2018.

"Theology Beer Camp: Birthday Edition." https://www.eventbrite.com/e/theology-beer-camp-birthday-edition-tickets-43485895484?aff=efbneb#.

Tillich, Paul. *Der Mut zum Sein*. 2nd ed. Berlin: de Gruyter, 2015.

―――. *Dynamics of Faith*. New York: HarperOne, 1957.

―――. *The Protestant Era*. Chicago: University of Chicago Press, 1948.

―――. *Systematic Theology*. Vol. 1. 3 vols. Chicago: University of Chicago Press, 1973.

―――. "Theology and Symbolism." In *Religious Symbolism*, edited by F. Ernest Johnson, 107–16. New York: Harper, 1955.

Troeltsch, Ernst. "Das stoisch-christliche Naturrecht und das moderne profane Naturrecht." In *Verhandlungen des 1. Deutschen Soziologentages vom 19. bis 22. Oktober 1910 in Frankfurt am Main*, by Deutsche Gesellschaft für Soziologie (DGS), 166–92. Frankfurt am Main: Sauer u. Auvermann, 1969.

Wagner-Rau, Ulrike, et al. "Pastoraltheologie." In *Praktische Theologie: Ein Lehrbuch*, edited by Kristian Fechtner et al., 105–27. Stuttgart: Kohlhammer, 2017.

Walter, Peter. "Priestertum." In *Enzyklopädie der Neuzeit Online*, edited by Friedrich Jaeger and Kulturwissenschaftliches Institut (Essen). Essen: Verlagsbuchhandlung and Poeschel, 2014.

Ward, Pete. *Introducing Practical Theology: Mission, Ministry, and the Life of the Church*. Grand Rapids: Baker Academic, 2017.

Wehner, Theo, and Stefan T. Güntert. *Psychologie der Freiwilligenarbeit: Motivation, Gestaltung und Organisation*. Berlin: Springer, 2015.

Williams, Rowan. *Being Disciples: Essentials of the Christian Life*. Grand Rapids: Eerdmans, 2016.

Wolff, Jürgen. "Sprachschule für die Freiheit, Option für die Armen oder perspektivenverschränkende Bildung?" In *Religiöse Erwachsenenbildung: Zugänge—Herausforderungen—Perspektiven*, edited by Isabelle Noth and Claudia Kohli Reichenbach, 27–44. 1st ed. Zürich: Theologischer Verlag Zürich, 2013.

Woodhead, Linda. "Introduction." In *Religion and Change in Modern Britain*, edited by Linda Woodhead and Rebecca Catto, 1–33. London: Taylor & Francis, 2012.

Young, Robert J. C. *Postcolonialism: An Historical Introduction*. Malden, MA: Wiley-Blackwell, 2001.

Zulehner, Paul. "Religion ja—Kirche nein? Die Kirche in der multikulturellen Gesellschaft von morgen." In *Kirche im 21. Jahrhundert: Vielfalt wird sein*, edited by Manfred Kock, 11–31. 1st ed. Stuttgart: Kreuz, 2004.

Zwingli, Ulrich. *Schriften*. Edited by Thomas Brunnschweiler et al. 4 vols. Zürich: Theologischer Verlag Zürich, 1995.